Gym Membership Sales

3x your growth, train your team, change your world

RYAN MOORE

ISBN: 978-1-7347281-0-1

Cover Design by 100Covers.com
Interior Design by FormattedBooks.com

Do not proceed without completing this step!

Before getting started, go to www.membershipsalesbook.com/ resources to create your free account and access the membership growth tools that go hand in hand with this book right now. This is different from a typical book that is easily read and forgotten. With this combination, you'll be fully equipped for measurable success in new membership growth in your gym or studio today.

Dedicated to my mom, dad and all of the mentors who have trained me in the things I'm sharing with you now. And to you, the new carrier of this information. I trust you'll use it to grow your business and ignite the leaders around you wherever you go.

CONTENTS

Introduction: Here's How to Get the Most Gym or Studio
Growth Out of This Book ix

Chapter 1   Four Concepts Unsuccessful Owners Miss 1
Chapter 2   Foundations for the Next Level 15
Chapter 3   Three Pillars 30
Chapter 4   What Kind of Owner are You? 37
Chapter 5   The Buyer's Journey 45
Chapter 6   Four Segment Sales System - Needs Assessment 56
Chapter 7   Four Segment Sales System - Packaging and
             Presentation 75
Chapter 8   Four Segment Sales System - Embracing
             Objections 82
Chapter 9   Four Segment Sales System -
             Onboarding and Retention 89
Chapter 10   Training Your Team 101
Chapter 11   Elite Communication 109
Chapter 12   Identifying or Creating an
             Elite Membership Salesperson 121

Epilogue: Sealing the Deal on Your Success 135

Here's How to Get the Most Gym or Studio Growth Out of This Book

"The people who are crazy enough to think they can change the world are the ones who do."
– Steve Jobs

Before Jessica doubled her membership revenue, she was struggling. In the weeks before we met, she had hardly added any members to her gym. That was a bad sign, and she knew it. There should be a lot of people joining this time of year, but they hadn't had a decent month in a while. But the rest all seemed right, she thought. Geat equipment, world class workouts, awesome staff, good location, friendly community... but her business was stagnant at best when it came to actually bringing in members (and profit).

It wasn't like Jessica had been sitting around hoping people would show up. She was working hard, trying her luck with one marketing company after another, boosting posts on social media, running ads on the local news channel, and all kinds of other strategies that didn't ever seem to work. Her gym wasn't growing, but her debt was—and so was her list of tasks. She knew that if something didn't change, it was only a matter of time...

That's when we started working together. Less than a month later, she had doubled her normal membership-growth rate. That taste of how things should be set her on a new trajectory, and over the next few months, her revenue doubled. A year later, everything about her life and business was completely different from how it looked before we met.

I've watched that happen hundreds of times with the fitness businesses I help. There's a spectrum of results, of course, but I've seen many do even *better* than Jessica.

The goal of this book is to achieve obvious and measurable success in the area of membership growth for a membership-based fitness business (like a gym or studio), resulting in increased time freedom for the owner. But before we start, I'm going to tell you exactly how this is done: the most successful owners take focused action on what matters most for the growth of their business each day and are adept at ignoring everything else.

It sounds easy to replicate, but it's not. Being motivated enough to focus on what matters most each day won't happen on it's own, and even then, while motivation is nice to have, it is not what matters most. The most successful people do *not* run on motivation alone. They use motivation when it's available, but their focus is on building habits instead of hoping to discover an untapped well of motivation. In this way, by default, the most important things get taken care of instead of the most motivating things, and distractions are stiff-armed on autopilot. The patterns you'll develop here will help you home in on what matters most and produce powerful, lasting results in your life and in your business.

Congratulations for choosing to invest in yourself and in your business by reading this book. I can't wait to hear about the lives you change, the new membership growth you experience, and the freedom you create in your own life along the way. Let's go!

CHAPTER ONE

Four Concepts Unsuccessful Owners Miss

"On any team, in any organization, all responsibility for success and failure rests with the leader. The leader must own everything in his or her world. There is no one else to blame. The leader must acknowledge mistakes and admit failures, take ownership of them, and develop a plan to win... There are no bad teams, only bad leaders."
– Jocko Willink, Extreme Ownership: How U.S. Navy SEALs Lead and Win

Our businesses and teams are extensions of who we, the owners, are as humans. They can't become something that the owner is not. Businesses tend to magnify our weaknesses and strengths, which is why avoiding feedback can feel great. On the other hand, owning the need for improvement is hard, but you've already gotten over that by making it this far. Well done. You've taken the first step toward having more members!

I've found that the best tools don't matter if what's happening under the surface isn't aligned with success. Success is what most people mistakenly aim for, but in reality, it's only the result of what's under the surface. The good news is that what we're about to explore in this segment will give you insight into four easily missed perspectives that most unsuccessful business owners are missing.

Don't move on to the next section until you've logged into the online resources that accompany this book. They are found at www. membershipsalesbook.com/resources.

Now that you've done that, you're ready to move on. Let's dive in!

Concept One: Ownership

A key indicator that a person is choosing to remain stuck in a situation is the presence of complaints. Anyone can grumble about anything; it's a perpetually readily available option. That is the seemingly easier path. Complaining about a thing feels better than taking responsibility for it and starts the process of transferring the blame for that thing to something outside of our control.

For instance, someone could say, "It's hard to get new members in through the doors. No one knows we're here!" This is what people call "venting," which is a nice way to say that someone is putting the energy of their frustration into complaining *instead of* into taking action. Ongoing complaints aid us in the construction of a particular perspective. One that makes sure a problem appears to be the fault of someone or something else. There's an instant reward for this. Deciding that something is not our fault and making sure it appears that way to others as well, feels great, in the moment. The cycle of self-placation and instant gratification is exactly what tries to hide our own responsibilities under layers of mental habits and ultimately keeps us stuck.

Instead of making the world feel instantly better by complaining, we could choose to take ownership of *our role* in it. We all have made decisions, consciously and unconsciously, that have brought us to exactly where we are.

Foregoing the complaints altogether takes a decision to deny ourselves the pleasure of deflecting, and instead leaves us with the responsibility to exercise ownership of the things that exist in our sphere. That is the seemingly harder path. When we choose not to complain and view it as our responsibility and no one else's, we begin looking that unpleasantness in the eye. From this stance, we get to choose if the thing is worth our attention at all. If it is not worth our attention, we can choose to stop wasting energy on it. If it is worth our attention, we can choose to do something about it. This grows our ability to ignore the unimportant and make our best attempt at influencing what is important. Habitually choosing ownership results in the development of strength, leading to more ownership and more strength and more influence on what matters most.

The decision to take ownership of everything that exists in our sphere, good and terrible, instantly results in higher levels of perceived influence. This contributes to the expectation that we are (and will continue to be) influential. This expectation leads to taking action in areas where we might not without the anticipation of success. Exercising that muscle of habitually taking action while anticipating success is what feeds personal effectiveness. Thus, the proclamation that you take ownership of everything that exists in your life leads to increased effectiveness, while assigning blame allows other influences to take the seat of authority. In every statement, belief, action, and habit we make, we are either feeding or starving our ability to influence our environment. Either way, the proclamation is fulfilled.

These things are binary. There are no habits that have a "neutral" effect. That is fairly obvious when seen from this perspective: A habit is either working for you or it is taking up the space of something that could be working for you. The problem is that in day-to-day operations, most people don't view all habits and choices as binary. We get around the challenge of identifying things as either good or bad by allowing the gray space of the "middle ground." This gives us a neutral place to put choices and habits we do not want to scrutinize. The belief that there is a "middle ground" is a pervasive trick that neutralizes more effective hours than the obvious, less common instances of gross ineffectiveness.

I invite you to take ownership of everything in your life for the rest of your life. Everything, as in: *Every. Single. Thing.* Leave no neutral ground and leave no room for shifting blame. Make your life and business a place where energy is invested in taking ownership, making decisions and producing solutions for what matters most. If it's not worth developing a solution for, it's not worth talking about.

Instead of aligning with helplessness, align with strength. You can identify opportunities for this whenever someone says something like, "It's so hard to ___ because of ___." For instance, if you were tempted to think, "It's so hard to add members because of the competition," recognize that it's not the competition's responsibility to provide you with instruction on how to beat them. They're not the responsible party—you are! Let's take ownership of the issue by taking a hard look at the fact that it is *you* who hasn't found a way to beat the competition.

If this happens to be something you've experienced, accepting sole responsibility for the situation might feel like salt in a wound. However, it does not make you weak to say that your situation is your responsibility. Assuming ownership of a situation is what makes you strong and puts you back into the seat of authority. Instead of allowing a casual complaint to slip out, pausing to choose ownership and looking an issue in the eye will give you a chance to speak a positive truth about your future.

Here's a statement of truth from a place of ownership in response to the exact same situation: "I'm in the process of overcoming competition. There is a way, and I'm finding it."

The moment you take bold ownership of your problems, in spite of the pain, is the moment you have the ability to influence them. When we complain about a thing, we're letting go of our authority in that area. Changing a thing all starts with ownership of the thing.

A common thread among successful business owners is this: They are the ones who solve others problems by choosing to take ownership of chaos and bring it to order. They make choices at a faster and more frequent rate than everyone else. They celebrate successes and continually train themselves to expect success. They outpace everyone who's afraid to try new things, given to overanalyzing due to fear of failure or stuck because they're blaming everything around them. Winners take action, expect success, and own the fact that they are the common thread to everything in their lives.

When we own who we really are, successes and failures are just experiences along the way and do not define us. In spite of how the moment you're in may look, I invite you to take relentless, fearless action and continually celebrate successes because that's what you're made for. This state of mind gives us freedom to take fearless action as a natural expression of who we are. In this way, you'll habitually operate from a state of success and enjoy the journey a lot more instead of continually struggling to get to some vague place of arrival. Instead of working to get *to* a place of strength and freedom, decide to operate *from* a place of strength and freedom right now.

Concept Two: Stop creating a job for yourself

Resolve today to stop creating a job for yourself. Instead, start creating systems and growing leaders. If you're spending most days on tasks related to the daily operations of your business or if you can't take a vacation for a few weeks without everything falling apart, it's time for a change. As your focus shifts away from creating a job for yourself, your expanded income, influence, and freedom will be the result of creating jobs for others. When the leaders you've grown can lead the people who run the systems you created, then you're ready to expand by multiplication instead of addition.

That all sounds great, but there are a few issues that might arise along the way. Here's the problem I ran into in the past: there's a lot more that can be done in a very short amount of time by *doing* more. But if you're putting in more effort to get more results, it will become unsustainable. As a business grows, the good and the bad grow together without apology.

More results from more effort can feel safe, because the familiar path is the one of least resistance for many of us. It's hard to invest energy in creating a refined solution that produces more results with less effort, especially if a dark, hidden corner part of our brain believes the lie that more results must come from more effort.

To shift out of the "more from more" mentality and into getting more results with less effort, begin noticing ways of creating systems and growing leaders instead of doing the work and accomplishing tasks.

Start by thinking through this process:

1.   Imagine something you spend effort on in your business that drains your energy, especially if it's repetitive and/or

time consuming. If you can't clearly identify something, start a time log until you can.

2. Think through the issue and attempt to identify the source of that thing—not the thing itself, but the root of it. Now, what's feeding the roots of that problem? Trace it all the way back to its fuel source. Eliminate the source itself, if possible. Don't fight a problem if you don't have to; cut off its supply instead, so the issue goes away on its own. If you can't identify the source or think of a way to cut the source off, try to imagine one to three completely crazy ways of addressing the situation. That imagination will open up your thoughts to more creative solutions.

3. If it truly is impossible to eliminate the source of the problem or situation, imagine a system that's set up so other people can handle it without you.

4. End by experiencing the feeling of success in this area: What would it be like to involve the people who would run your business in the development of that new system? Eventually, would it be possible for some of those people to grow into leaders who could originate or iterate on your designs and create or refine systems for you? What impacts might that have on your life? What about their lives?

The difference between growing by putting in more effort and growing by creating systems and helping others develop is the difference between progressing toward freedom and progressing toward bondage.

In light of that, take pride in how few things are on your "to do" list, not on how many things you can accomplish in a day. Those with shorter lists have done harder work of focusing their effort on things that matter most. Show me someone with a list of twenty items on their list of action items for the day, and I'll show you someone who doesn't know how to prioritize their investment of time and energy on the things that matter most.

Never, ever brag about how many hours you work. Instead, be proud of yourself for producing higher-level solutions that work for you without your time and effort. Up to a certain point, more effort does produce more results. But then we reach a point of diminishing returns where more units of effort do not produce the same return of results. Once that point is reached, we have to shift into a different mentality. Many people get stuck here, because successfully making that shift means letting go of the exact way of thinking that got us to that point. But once the point of diminishing returns is reached, working more is not the same as being more effective and having more impact. The world doesn't need the most exhausted, stretched-thin, tired, and tattered version of you. Your business, team, and customers need the *best* version of you. When you're at your best is when you're most effective.

As your business and impact grow, so will the positive or negative effects of your decisions and state of mind. So, for any business owner who's reached the point of diminishing returns for their own effort, living your life from the place of maximum effectiveness comes from focusing on these things:

- Recovering and resting well so you're equipped to make the best decisions
- Progressing in your ability to create systems and solutions that run without your personal effort
- Becoming better at identifying and completing the few things that matter most

Concept Three: Seek the simplest solution

I used to love fancy solutions, until I relearned a few lessons on how powerful simplicity is. The summer I turned eleven, a great friend of mine inspired me to read a book called *The American Boy's Handy Book*. It was a guide for just about everything a boy could ask for. I learned things like making kites by hand, woodworking, survival in the wild, and how to make slingshots.

That summer, I spent basically forever perfecting a live box-trap. My plan was to catch squirrels, frogs, and birds in the field behind my house. Who knew, maybe I'd even catch my sister's rabbit (the one my parents probably gave away but assured us at the time that it had "escaped").

Whatever was out there, I aimed to capture it. I had planned to decide what to do with whatever I caught once I could properly assess how to keep it based on things like size, strength, and aggressiveness. After that, I would tell my mother about what I caught, but only if it was so big or noisy that there was absolutely no way to keep it a secret.

Catching creatures from the unknown turned out to present some significant challenges. The mechanism for keeping the trap door closed after an intelligent animal was in it seemed like it would elude me forever.

I tested one "brilliant" solution after another, none of which resulted in the box actually retaining an animal for further inspection. After at least a thousand weeks of failure that summer, I knew I had to start thinking bigger. I decided it was time to consult my dad. This was something of a risk, because it seemed possible to me that he would disapprove of my venture and put an end to it, but I was left with no options. So, I lurked around the front yard, waiting to hear his work truck growling up the street.

The afternoon wore on as I stayed faithful to the important tasks at hand. We had been digging for the bones of our dead hamster for some time so I had employees to manage (also known as sisters). I was running a tight security detail in the backyard to maintain a bee-free environment. That helped keep my employees safe and productive. In addition to that, the supply of tablespoons from my mother's silverware drawer (our "shovels") seemed to be running thin. So, besides watching the front yard, managing the dig site and the security detail, I had to secure the digging implements. We couldn't risk the entire program on someone who didn't have experience getting tablespoons undetected, so that had to be me.

As the day wore on, the shadows lengthened, and I finally heard Dad's truck pulling into the driveway. It was time to seize the moment of opportunity...

I dashed around the corner of the house, through the gate, holding my breath past garbage cans that were sweltering in the summer sun and into the carport. My dad was just getting to the back of his truck. I blurted, "Hi Dad!" and so began my epic pitch. He patiently waited at the back door of the truck in his sweaty, sawdust-covered clothes to hear my long explanation, which crescendoed into the epic solution: he should fix the trap for me. He might even do it right then and there! If I did my job right, I'd have a new employee any second.

"Hmm, let me think about that," he pondered, furrowing his brow.

To my dismay, instead of dropping everything and providing the epic solution, he slowly began to unload the truck.

As I watched him take a few trips back and forth, he said, "Why don't you help me unload the truck? There's a broom and dustpan there in the corner."

Foiled! My whole plan had gone wrong. I wasn't getting any help at all, and now I had even more challenges to face. Hesitating there for a moment, I narrowed my eyes at the broom, and re-assessed a new angle to achieve my goal. Seeing that the only path was forward, I began to jab at the floor of the truck with the broom, making clouds of dust billow out all around me as I did so. They looked to me like tendrils of smoke highlighted in the golden rays of the setting sun. Dad didn't think so, and I promptly received a lesson on how to sweep properly.

It took *forever*, especially with having to wield the broom so gently, but three or four minutes later, we had finished cleaning out the truck. I saw my chance and, in a flicker of hope, piped, "What about now?"

All I got was a puzzled look. I waited, dumbfounded, wondering how Dad could somehow forget what was really important here. Realizing what I meant, he said, "Oh yes, the trap... Let me think about that."

I knew what that meant. He'd amble in after the long day's work, kiss my mother, take a shower, and eat dinner. Then he would probably attend to a series of household chores or business paperwork before settling in. I went to the backyard to think about what had gone wrong.

Later that evening, we talked about the trap at the dinner table, and after dinner he set everything aside and helped me build the complicated latch I wanted. I was so eager to see it work that I spent all night dreaming of great adventures.

"Who knows," I mused, "I might even catch a coyote...."

The next morning, the bait had been taken, but the empty trap told the same story. That evening, I listed all the possible problems at the back of Dad's truck again.

My dad is a man of many thoughts and few words, so when he speaks, he usually shares things of deep value. That day, he didn't fix my trap like I wanted. He just quietly said, "Son, sometimes the simplest solutions are the best."

He knew that what I—and probably his sanity—needed was more than a quick fix. The best solution was not going to be found in an elaborate scheme. That was a conclusion I needed to reach on my own. It produced some interesting results that I'll tell you more about later on....

My Dad's quiet statement that day has become a theme that echoes through my life. I've discovered that anyone can create a complex house of cards, but it takes time and a rare sort of dedication to create the simple systems that can stand the test of time.

Pursuing the simplest possible solutions to resolve complex challenges with the least amount of effort is what produces resilient systems that are worth replicating. This is a lesson from a page out of my dad's legacy that our buzzing world could get a lot out of. You won't be floating along with the current if you seek the simplest solutions, but it will be worth it.

Secret Four: Time

> *"My favorite things in life don't cost any money. It's really clear that the most precious resource we all have is time." – Steve Jobs*

Gym Membership Sales

You get to choose what to do with the most precious resource available in the entire world: time. People who can be caught saying, "There's not enough time," are unhealthy in one of the worst ways. The truth is that time is not in lack, because there's never any less or more of it. There's never more time than you can use, and there's never not enough of it. Time is a free gift. It is the great equalizer of all people. From the richest to the poorest, we all have the exact same amount of seconds, minutes, and hours each day.

Time is the most valuable resource and 100 percent of it must be invested, spent, or passed each day. How you do that is completely up to you.

Achieving anything in life is more about what you remove from your life than what you add. Throw your TV away. Delete social media apps. Don't spend time with people who aren't urging you forward. Instead of shifting blame by saying, "There's not enough time," take ownership of your time. Do the harder work of eliminating first, automating second, and delegating third. Just to get your wheels turning, here are some examples of a few simple things I've eliminated from my life that returned significant dividends:

- Weekly shows and news media of all sorts
- Following politics and engaging in political arguments, especially online
- Notifications on apps
- The grocery store
- Unimportant decisions, chores, and errands

I've successfully avoided the grocery store for years by having the same order of groceries delivered to my house each week. I place a high value on having a clean and orderly environment, but by refusing to spend time on chores and errands, I'm forced to pay people who are happy to earn an income doing those things. I choose to perceive those costs as an investment, both in people and in the ability to reallocate that time to things that produce income or progress for me, my clients, and my team.

You can fight distraction, of course. But what if there's a simpler solution? Here's an oversimplified example: I don't typically put people in my inner circle of friends who spend every free weekend getting drunk downtown. I used to love bar hopping with friends, but I no longer find that to be the best investment of time. I *could* spend effort fighting the desire to stay out later for another beer, just like fighting the temptation to spend time scrolling a newsfeed, or checking one more notification, but I've found if I remove the opportunity for distraction to exist at all, the effort I would have spent resisting it can be invested in more valuable things. For that reason, I've stopped notifications on all devices and removed nearly all apps from the home screen of my phone.

The more decision-making energy we reserve for the decisions that matter most and the more money we spend in order to save time that otherwise would have been spent on tasks, the more we're encouraged to pass our time well. This supports the development of habits that reorient our energy to produce progress, rather than letting the majority of our energy be absorbed by distractions, routine operations, and maintenance. Time passes by default, so structure your habits to support investing energy in advancing into new territory and bring order to chaos by default.

CHAPTER TWO

Foundations for the Next Level

"Both poverty and riches are the offspring of thought."
– Napoleon Hill, Think and Grow Rich

There's not much in life that matters more than choosing and crafting your mindset. By far, the biggest success factor is mindset. It's more important than having the best sales skills, the newest equipment, low competition, or a great location.

You don't have to take my word for it, because this thought stands the test of reason. Mentality impacts every single aspect of someone's life, and the business is just an extension of the person. I'd always invest in someone with mediocre tools and the best mentality over someone with the best tools and mediocre mentality. In this chapter, we're going to discuss what some of the most important elements of a powerful mentality look like.

Winner's Mentality

Winner's Mentality is a state of being, a perspective with which to approach the world around us. It's a type of footing from which we can choose to interface with the chaos around us. Winners approach situations from a place of confidence. They operate as if they have already won. They see success *before* the battle begins, and if they are struggling to find this place in their mind, they force themselves to go there. If they can't do that, they know to at least *act* like a winner, outwardly. They know that if they can force their body into moving like a winner, their Winner's Mentality is likely to follow.

Culture is what transfers this Winner's Mentality from you to your staff, clients, and entire business. The question is, how do you build a Winner's Mentality, and how do you build it into the culture of your business?

Let's imagine a team member or colleague who is responsible for sales. This person is friendly, a good listener, passionate, and confident. A person like that should naturally be great at sales, but that doesn't mean they will be. We've all seen someone struggle to make sales when it seems like they're the kind of person who shouldn't. There are several reasons this can happen:

1. They don't have motivation.
2. They don't believe in their own ability to sell.
3. They don't believe in the value of what they are selling.

These problems are all due to not having a Winner's Mentality. As leaders, we are the ones who have to teach our staff how to both create and maintain their Winner's Mentality.

The goal is for you and everyone on your team to click into a victorious state before you interface with challenge. Keep in mind that you cannot call another person up into a state of strength without already being there yourself.

You'll occasionally hear sales-oriented cultures use the term, "on fire." It's often used to describe a salesperson who is on a winning streak of sale after sale. Why do sales often come in winning streaks? It has less to do with the quality of the prospect and a lot more to do with the mental footing of the salesperson. Cultivate the ability to step into this Winner's Mentality, no matter how many "no's" or cancellations you encounter.

Habitually and intentionally frequenting the Winner's Mentality until it is the natural way of being is the direction to grow in. A simple way to condition this state is to make a habit of regularly drawing out and celebrating wins of any sort until it becomes the cultural norm. I like to ask questions like:

- What are you celebrating this week?
- What's something great that happened today?
- What are you looking forward to?

These are questions you can try practicing at the grocery store before you try them out on your team. It will be fun! (As a side note, practicing gratitude has the same effect because it conditions our normal state into one of looking for things to feel great about.)

One of the benefits of cultivating the Winner's Mentality is that we'll become better at asking prospects deeper questions in search of things to celebrate. Once we know what goals a prospect has in mind, we hear not just what a prospect wants to achieve but how someone's life will be impacted by the achievement of those things. The prospect has to first imagine the success before they'll be able to list the impacts. This will help the prospect slip into a Winner's Mentality of their own. Hope is a powerful drug. If someone can't imagine a thing and hope for it, they're not going to be able to achieve it.

This emotional shift is powerful not just for the prospect, but for the salesperson as well. Hearing a shallow, "I want to tone up" goal does not bring the prospect into a Winner's Mentality or help them apprehend the value of what journey they're considering embarking

Ryan Moore

on. A shallow goal also does not give the salesperson much to celebrate when that member joins.

This focus on celebrating before a battle has started is powerful, and not just for making the sale but for doing the deeper work of changing a life from the inside out. This way, the sale happens because the prospect is being, acting, and choosing from a new state. Buying a membership is just a natural byproduct of a new internal state.

An easy way to coach this way of selling is to teach your salespeople that both they and the prospect should achieve the Winner's Mentality, the place where they both feel as if the victory was already won. They both should operate out of confidence. This helps the salesperson remain happy for the success of the prospect rather than hungry for commission, while helping the prospect truly understand the deeper benefits of the membership.

Will clients still fall off the path? Yes, they will. Will salespeople miss sales they should have closed? Yes, they will. The right mindset alone will not fix everything, but when our team's Winning Mindset focuses on the people we can help, we will change more lives than we ever thought possible.

Achieving this mindset is easier said than done. Trauma, negativity, and unfortunate circumstances are more significant in our brains than wins are. No one talks about how many cars they saw driving safely on their way to work. They only remember the mangled wreck on the side of the road.

That's why it's our responsibility to influence the mentality of our teams toward a state of presence, safety, success, clarity, confidence, and freedom. This is done, in part, through methodical collection and internal distribution of success stories in our businesses, which

18

can be summed up by the label, "celebrating success." Problems will always scream for attention. It's our job to shift the focus to the successes. We are the ones who must establish a Winner's Mentality, and we will see more lives changed and more sales made as a result.

I'm going to give you a specific path for achieving this with prospects later on. For now, just understand that inspiring a Winner's Mentality in your prospects matters and it can't be forced or contrived. For that to be natural, we must be practiced at intentionally cultivating Winner's Mentality within ourselves first, our teams second and our members third.

This Winner's Mentality concept should not be new, but if it's not what you preach on the regular, your team will not absorb it. Winner's Mentality is an intentionally developed habit.

Don't focus on the sale

Most people, when trying to close a sale, focus on making the sale. That's a great way to ruin your chance. Focusing on a future moment reduces the ability to absorb the present moment. Even when the sale may feel "in the bag" to the salesperson, it may not feel that way to the prospect. Sales can be totally lost when on the edge of success.

When present focus is reduced, we are more likely to lose rapport, miss details, or fail to draw out their hesitations. This loss of presence can also trigger sales resistance, which happens when someone feels pressure to buy. Everyone likes to buy, but people don't like to be sold to. When a prospect notices that what we care about is the sale, it gets translated as lack of care for them. When that happens, your chance is often lost.

Being attached to the future outcomes of your present actions is the root of this loss of focus. Besides reducing focus, it can also produce anxiety.

Anxiety comes from concern about a future moment. At the core, anxiety is a kind of faith in the thought that the future contains something bad. The easiest way to stop anxiety is to remain present. The easiest way to remain present is to release the fear-based urge to manage the future.

There's enough to grapple with today without inviting the problems of tomorrow to gang up on us as well.

Imagine if every potential member we spoke to had no self-doubt from the past or the future clouding their brains, only a clear understanding of where they are now and where they'd like to go. It would be easier to help that kind of person make a clear decision than someone afflicted with self-doubt and worry.

Being the person who invests in these state-of-mind habits gives us the chance to help others, like prospects and employees, operate in this state, too. The teams we lead will close better when they, too, cultivate the habit of remaining present. Our teams will have more clarity, be better listeners, and handle the present better than they would in a state distracted by worry. This leads to increased likelihood of success in all areas. Repetition of success results in increases in confidence and decisiveness. Clarity, confidence, and increased decisiveness will make your team better equipped to invite prospects to join them in that state.

Separating sleeze from sales

Someone might have used a barbell to break down a door and steal things, but just because a tool can be used for evil doesn't make the tool itself evil. If the word "sales" represents negative things to you, it's time to let that go. Some people will use sales for things they shouldn't. But that's not who you are.

Our role is to help people make progress beyond their current situation and into a brighter future. When hurdles arise, we'll be helping people make a decision without being pushy. Do not confuse pushing someone to a decision with being good at sales. Pushiness is not something elite salespeople use.

Let's start by clarifying what a healthy salesperson is. The role of a salesperson is not to push a person into a choice, but rather to guide a person through the shadows of doubt that naturally arise when making a decision.

The truth is that nearly everyone hesitates at the edge of a decision. It's a basic survival instinct to do your best to mitigate risk, but hesitating does not serve progression toward your ultimate goal. It only slows or halts this progression.

A good salesperson knows this and allows a prospective client to move toward a choice one small step at a time. They help prospects reach a new state of mind and make confident choices. They do not allow people to hesitate in fear or get trapped in stagnation.

With this strategy, the prospect ultimately decides for themselves. When the shift into this mentality occurs, the ripple effect that sales are meant to have begins. When a salesperson is fulfilling their calling, they lead others to a new state of mind that makes buying memberships, making referrals, and achieving long-term results happen naturally. Elite salespeople know that a prospect's shift toward a fitter future comes from the new state of mind.

"The journey of a thousand miles begins with
a single step." — J. R. R. Tolkien.

What are we selling?

Investment of time and energy into something only happens if we find it important to begin with, but the more time and energy gets invested into something, the more likely we are to keep pouring more into it. The more we pour into it, the more of ourselves is in it. The more of ourselves that is in it, the more we value it and want to talk about it.

Here's an illustration for you. Someone, let's call him Joe, sees a car with one of those, "My Child is an Honor Student...Again!" bumper stickers.

Joe finds this sticker to be self-absorbed and boastful, especially when Joe considers that the motivation for purchasing this bumper sticker is not really about championing the success of the child; it's much more self-centered than that. The real motivator for buying that bumper sticker is self-promotion on the part of the "successful" parent.

Therefore, Joe becomes motivated to buy the, "My Kid Beat Up Your Honor Student...Again" bumper sticker. Maybe it's purchased in jest, as a way of making fun of self-centered parenting, or maybe it's bought out of feeling threatened by the success of others. Either way, the purchase of this bumper sticker is reactionary and defensive.

There's nothing wrong with championing success, but there is something wrong with *needing* to champion success. The first parent, if they were truly secure, wouldn't have felt a need for self-promotion. Joe, if he was truly secure, wouldn't have felt threatened by the success of others.

This is what happens with our product. We are the ones interested in workouts because they are a part of us. Prospects, on the other hand, aren't actually interested in workouts. They don't care that your gym equipment has Italian leather made by the same company Ferrari uses. That's what we, in the industry, care about. Prospects also don't want to hear about how great your classes are. That's what you and your instructors want to hear about.

New employees or those unsure of the value of the product will tend toward self-promotion, but having everyone think the product is great is not the actual goal of a sales conversation. What we're actually trying to do is produce action on the part of the prospect. We want to shift them from the path they are on to the path that will take them where they'd like to be. That's the goal. We do not make sales and change lives by trying to force prospects into thinking our product is great. Instead, we do this by helping them see that our product is the vehicle for getting them to where they'd like to go.

Remember, we're asking someone to take time out of their day to lift heavy things, stretch, or pedal a bike. We're inviting them to put themselves through physical pain. We're offering few short-term benefits in a world that's oriented to expect immediate reward. If they stick with it long enough, it's possible that they might experience some benefits, but in the meantime, they work, sweat, experience pain, and sacrifice their time—and *we're* the ones getting paid for it!

No, prospects are not interested in a workout. Think one layer deeper. People will put themselves through pain for the achievement of their goals. That's closer. Achievement of goals is what prospects will *say* they want. However, the achievement of the goals is not what they are *actually* after.

Focusing on the goals will also not reliably produce a sale, especially not in the life of someone who is not already in the habit of working out. Prospects are already aware of the logical reasons for working out: better sleep, better body, better sex, more energy, more confidence, etc. Even though the goals they have in mind and the logical reasons for working out are what a prospect says they want, goals and benefits of working out will not produce action. That's because the achievement of goals is not actually what the prospect wants.

How do we know that the results of working out isn't what a prospect wants? Because emotion trumps logic every time. Desperately needing to be in better shape but being held back by the emotional fear of being judged will stop someone in their tracks. This is why some choose the pain of remaining the same over the pain of working out. It's also why people will say, "I need to get in better shape before I can join a gym." The fear of being judged carries more weight than the inevitable health concerns of tomorrow. When the mind weighs the pros and cons of taking action today, it acts on feelings. Typically, fear will sound something like, "I need to talk with my spouse first," or "I want to think about it." Keep in mind that *not* making a choice is adding to the habits of yesterday. Not making a choice is what's been keeping someone stuck before they came in. Saying "maybe" is the same as saying, "I'm not going to take any action at all and will continue as I was."

Think about it—we've all seen the person who needs to take action but doesn't. It's frustrating when someone doesn't take action, especially when we see that our product will have a massive impact on their life. The prospects aren't stupid; they see that too. The problem is that the core drivers for producing action are several layers under the surface. If we are focused on the impacts, our aim is off. If we are aiming at the wrong target, the prospects will too. The drivers that move a prospect toward obvious benefits are not found in benefits themselves. They are located one layer deeper.

The drivers are not the achievements. The drivers are the feelings that come with the achievements.

Look for motivators, not reasons

Feelings overpower logic every time. If I should lose weight because I'm eating myself into an early grave, that's a great *reason* to take action. However, it's not a *motivator*. Logical reasons and motivators are different.

Reasons look like:

- Getting off of blood pressure medication
- Living a higher quality of life
- Having better sleep

Motivators look like:

- The feeling of satisfaction that comes with fitting into the little black dress
- The warmth someone feels when thinking about being able to play with their grandchildren. How their heart feels, knowing they are doing their best to be active for years to come. In contrast, how they feel when thinking about being stuck on the couch instead of playing with the kids on the floor.
- Avoiding the feeling of shame between the parking lot and the door to the XXXL store or the feeling of confidence that comes with having a healthy exterior

Emotions trump logic, and emotions are complicated. If logic was stronger or if emotions were simpler, sales would be easy. If logic closed sales, people would walk in and we'd say, "What do you want to achieve? Is that worth $150 per month? Okay, sign here."

That rarely works, because emotions spark each other and run all over the landscape of our minds, waking other emotions up, each with their own voices and goals. I've seen this story play out on the face of thousands of prospects as they found themselves considering progress:

One day, as Prospect thought about working out, Logic spoke to her:

"Join the cycle studio. Get in shape. You're dying faster with all this extra weight. Enough is enough."

"But what if everyone there is in great shape and you're the only fat one?" questioned Insecurity.

Apathy remembered how Prospect turned aside so easily last time Prospect visited a gym. All he had to whisper was, "What if you *do* join the cycle studio, but you do it another day? Tomorrow is so much better." And Apathy added, in a voice dripping with sugary sweetness, "It would feel so much nicer to just get some extra sleep today. Wouldn't it?" Apathy knew from experience that Logic was determined, so he followed that up with a little peace offering. Smiling a toothy grin, he said, "That way you'll wake up totally energized and ready to get started!"

Logic, ever resilient, said loudly, "You'll only be fatter tomorrow. Putting this off isn't helping—"

"What! That's exactly what your brother used to say!" Insecurity blurted out.

Then, in a dark tone dripping with malice, Bitterness spat, "Yes, you don't need people like that in your life."

Stubbornness, Bitterness's twin brother, had put a lot of effort into keeping the family members apart. So he elbowed his way in and said, "Yep, there's no way you should forgive him for that." Then, narrowing his squinty eyes, he queried Prospect, saying, "You're not that weak, are you?"

On and on it went, and the voice of Logic was easily lost in the clamor. Fear, Insecurity, Apathy, Stubbornness, and Bitterness had won. This is how things went in Prospect's brain for several weeks. Then, one day, the pain of remaining the same overcame the pain of fear.

She dragged her heavy head to the studio and was shown around by an impossibly fit instructor. He helped her set up her bike in the back. Barely making it through the class without throwing up, Prospect couldn't wait to get out of there. Just before she made it to the door, one of the people who worked at the studio shouted, "I heard you did really well in class!" Before Prospect could ask how this person knew her, he said, "This is the best studio in town. We have the most up-to-date equipment. The best instructors are here, and everyone displays their results on the TV. Check out these new heart rate monitors. They're the best in the business!" His bouncy enthusiasm was a little annoying to Prospect, who felt like she was teetering on the verge of dying.

But she was polite and allowed him to go on talking about how their studio was "the best" for the next few minutes. As Prospect stood there, wishing she wasn't struggling to remain standing, her patience grew thinner as her limbs grew shakier.

She listened as long as she could, not wanting to be rude. Then, she finally came up with an excuse to leave, and said, "Okay, great. I really loved it here, but I have to pick my kids up soon."

The bouncy guy then said, "Okay, let's get you on your way, pronto! Here are our membership options. I think you should do a twelve-month commitment so that we can make sure you get to your goals."

The voices of Apathy and past failures began to overwhelm Prospect's thoughts. She smiled thinly and said, "Great, I'll run all this by my husband and get back to you guys tomorrow. I really have to get on the road. Do you have something I can take with me?"

Most of the time, when someone doesn't make a decision in the moment, no changes happen. Prospect didn't join the next day, because she was sore. The next day, she had plans in the evening. The day after that came and went, as Bitterness reminded her of how much that guy had sounded like her brother. The week came and went, as well as the next month and year.

This pattern went on, until one day, the pain of the current situation pushed her in through the door of your business. This team wasn't allowed to be self-absorbed in their product. They were trained to change lives instead of selling memberships. So, instead of your team member saying, "These are the best pieces of equipment around," they said something like, "What kinds of things would you like to achieve if you were to start working out?" Then when Prospect said she'd like to tone up, they responded, "Okay, and what other areas of your life could be affected if you were to 'tone up'?"

The quiet confidence of your team member woke something different in Prospect's heart this time. In the stillness, instead of fear-based Insecurity and Apathy, Confidence was given space to speak. Prospect quietly said, "I guess I'd be able to fit in the clothes I used to wear." There was a bit of a pause and she went on to say, "I'd also probably have a little more energy."

The team member smiled, asked a few more questions and allowed the feeling of confidence to permeate the atmosphere. Then, exuding a peaceful strength, the team member said, in a measured tone, "So, if you were to work out consistently for a few months and found yourself having more energy, fitting in the clothes you used to wear, what would that do for you?"

"It would help me set a better example for my kids," said Prospect.

"And if you felt like you were setting a better example for your kids, what would that be like?" For the first time in a long time, Joy spoke up in Prospect's mind, saying, "That would feel so incredible. You'd be elated!" And, just like that, a real smile broke across Prospect's face.

As a sales expert, you'll notice the difference. In the first place, they were pushing the product into focus and talking about how cool they were. In the second place, they asked questions and the prospect did almost all the talking. They unearthed the reasons for taking action but didn't stop there. They pressed in past the goals, reasons and logic to draw out the motivators. Knowing that feelings outweigh reasons every time, they made their target several layers deeper. They went for what the prospect was really after: the feelings that would come with achieving the goals.

As an expert sales trainer in the making, you'll want this to happen by default. The target is to discover the motivators, and the path to doing that is much easier than you might think. By the end of this book, you'll have the tools to condition this ability into your team.

CHAPTER THREE

Three Pillars

"Make sure every day you do what matters most.
When you know what matters most, everything makes sense. When
you don't know what matters most, anything makes sense."
– Gary Keller, The One Thing: The Surprisingly
Simple Truth Behind Extraordinary Results

A fitness business rests on three pillars. The first is marketing. The second is sales. The third is retention. Everything will fail if just one pillar is missing (though there is one that matters more than the others). Let's briefly explore each of them.

Retention

For most fitness business owners, this looks like focusing on the product:

- Buying new, high-quality stationary bikes, boxing bags, and other equipment
- Keeping the facility clean and in great repair
- Providing extras, like towel service
- Having the right floors for weightlifting, Olympic lifting, functional training, or cardio classes
- Paying attention to the atmosphere, the color scheme, the music, and overall member experience

Lots of fitness business owners over-prioritize the product and fail because of it. It's so easy to slip into this trap, because the product is the most tangible portion of the business. The blue wall that would look better in light tan stares us in the face each day. The image of our less-than-cutting-edge stationary equipment arrests our thoughts every time we see the newest studio down the street.

Besides this, the product is the portion of the business many of us are most familiar with. Trainers, coaches, and group fitness instructors are all oriented to over-emphasize the product in this way. Interestingly enough, leaning on the apparent strength of our product can inadvertently create weakness in other crucial areas that won't surface right away.

Don't bank on the greatness of your product. In most fitness businesses, excluding the very inexpensive options, retention is mostly produced by less tangible elements than the physical product. But we'll talk about those later on.

Most people who don't own businesses think that if you build a really, *really* good product, people will just show up. I have seen beautiful hopes, dreams, and intentions come to nothing because of that mindset. Several of my own early businesses were dashed to fragments on the harsh rocks of this reality.

I still remember the first time I paused to think about this concept. I was selling gym memberships, involved primarily in management and revenue growth. I always noticed new gyms and often stopped in to visit them. This particular day, I was driving slowly through San Diego, enjoying the sunshine. As the palm trees whisked by the passenger window, I noticed a new gym.

It stood out to me because it was positioned perfectly. It was located on one of the busiest corners in an area full of fit people, and everyone in walking distance easily had enough money to afford their boutique membership rates. On top of that, at the time, there weren't any decent gyms in that area. I walked in, checked it out, talked with a few people, and met the owner.

The owner was a great guy with a great heart and a well-known product. He had all the certifications, training experience, and financial backing. He had no real direct competition and brand-new equipment. What could go wrong? Knowing what revenue numbers were easily within their reach with just two to three hundred members, I stepped back out into the sunshine, already thinking about how different things would be when I visited next.

Fast forward a few months. As the summer sun started to warm things up, I found myself driving through that neighborhood again on the way to a great surfing spot. As I smiled over at the corner where the gym used to be, I saw a row of shiny, beach-cruiser bicycles. Confusion gave way to dismay. The gym was no longer there. I began to process the shock. That awesome gym was in the perfect location. How could this have happened? It was a sure thing! The owner had heart and a great product. At the time, I thought that it must have been some odd stroke of poor luck. There was no way he could have failed otherwise...

That was the first fitness business I had followed from inception to demise. I began to dig deeper to figure out why it had failed when it seemed it shouldn't have. That curiosity eventually led to connections with thousands of fitness business owners.

Most fitness businesses fail within their first few years. The most common reason for this is that they didn't sell enough memberships to become profitable before the owner's money ran out. The rate of membership growth is the killer in most scenarios.

Gym Membership Sales

You may be wondering, "If this kind of business failure is so predictable, why don't people see it before it happens?" Consider this: A group exercise instructor, personal trainer, or yoga teacher develops a strong following. Eventually, they get sick of hustling. Long hours and terrible pay, often with no benefits, gets pretty old. They decide it's time to open their own business. They figure if they keep providing a great product and own the business, it won't take long to get it off the ground. They do the math and realize they only need fifty clients to break even. They open their business, and what they know is what they focus on. They don't consider marketing; they figure the clients will come. And when they don't, their business closes, and they're left in an even worse place financially than before.

Thinking like you used to think is just enough to keep you where you were. You'll have to think new thoughts to be somewhere you've never been.

That story is way too common. But there's another category of fitness business owners. Take, for instance, one of my clients— let's call her Sally. It was her goal to open at a profit. I helped her with the pre-sale for her studio, and she opened with a reasonably strong start. She had over $25,000 worth of automatically recurring monthly membership revenue *before* she opened her doors. This was in the type of facility where her overhead can remain under $15,000 per month. Instead of hoping the membership revenue caught up to her expenses, she went after what was possible. She didn't wait until she desperately needed more members to focus on membership growth. She started focusing on membership growth as her only priority and was selling memberships well before opening. She had never owned a gym before and didn't know how to do that at first, but she knew it was possible. By seeing what was possible, her brain went to work on filling in the resources for that possibility—and so, she found the right people to accomplish the job.

What makes the difference in these two types of owners? Instead of focusing on fulfillment and her product, Sally focused on what produces a successful business. She invested in marketing and making sales over everything else. Now, no matter what fulfillment challenges come along, she has the money to fix it. It's easy for her product to be the best because she can afford the best equipment and the best instructors. Even though sales, marketing, and fulfillment all support each other, a sustainable product is the result of sustainable sales and marketing. It might sound odd at first, but prioritizing sales and marketing is what produces the best product in the long run.

Marketing

I always hear, "We need more leads!" The problem is that leads don't always produce memberships. A lead is several steps away from a membership, but it's easy to think that marketing will naturally solve a lack of memberships. The thought goes like this: If more people just knew we were here, it would be so much easier. But where does that leave you if increased leads do not result in increased memberships?

Leads are close to the goal, but they are not the goal. The actual goal is membership growth. There are a few steps between the lead and the long-term happy member. Things like following up with a new lead, booking their appointment, and making sure they show up. This is what I call "lead nurturing." Then there's the sales process, which usually requires a different set of skills for leads from advertising than it does for leads who come in on their own. Often, other gym and studio owners have told me they worked with a company who did advertising for them, but, "The leads were terrible." Usually, the leads were deemed terrible because most of them didn't show up and most of the leads who did never joined. That could be a marketing issue, but it's much more likely to be a lead-nurturing issue. Fixing the lead nurturing might change everything, but it probably won't, because if there's a lead-nurturing issue, there's usually also a sales issue.

At the end of the day, it's our job to have systems in place to make sure the leads show up in our gyms and studios. It's up to us to take ultimate responsibility for the show ratio of the leads that marketers generate and from all other sources. Do not look for a marketer to bring you the magic potion that produces a successful gym. No one is coming to save your business. The person who is going to save your business is already here, reading this book.

Sales

It's easy to scapegoat marketing in a scenario where a business is acquiring leads yet not making sales, but if leads are expressing interest and sharing accurate contact information, the marketing *is* working. If the marketing is working but the leads aren't coming in, it's a lead-nurturing problem. If they are coming in but they aren't joining, it's a sales problem. If they are joining but not staying for a year or more and regularly referring friends, it's a retention problem. Lead nurturing only matters when marketing is going well. Marketing is only sustainable when sales are happening as a result.

Retention and referrals don't get to happen at all without sales. That is why sales is the one pillar that matters most. Sales is the lynchpin, not marketing, because sales has the greatest impact on all other aspects of the business. It doesn't matter how good the marketing is or how good the product is if the business isn't closing membership sales. When you make sales the priority, everything else in the business is easier and better for it.

If the sales process is strong, however, it makes sense to market. When sales and marketing are strong, there's more than enough revenue to provide a great product and invest in things like new equipment and aesthetics.

Remember, new paint or equipment won't produce new leads on its own without marketing, marketing will not sustain itself without a very strong sales process, and there will be no members to retain without sales. They are all three important, of course. Knowing the relationship between the three matters, too. But without sales, there is no revenue. Without revenue, there is no business. So, if you get something wrong in your business, don't let it be something in the sales process. The second tier of priority would be the things most immediately related to the point of sale, like the lead-nurturing process before and the onboarding process right after. The third tier contains all things that feed the sales process, like marketing and visibility measures. When these things are done well, the product will take care of itself.

CHAPTER FOUR

What Kind of Owner are You?

"My friend...care for your psyche...know thyself, for once we know ourselves, we may learn how to care for ourselves."
– Socrates

In this segment, I'm going to identify three types of owners and two types of leads. You'll likely fall primarily into one category of owner but be able to learn something from all of them. Taking a good assessment of where you are is the first step in moving beyond where you have been.

The Fitness Pro

This is the owner who has spent time servicing fitness clients in the past before starting their own business. Usually, it's their own product, not a franchise. They grow a modest membership base pretty soon after opening without much advertising. Often, the businesses are primarily built on organic leads and member referrals. They usually don't become profitable before opening with a pre-sale strategy.

The product is what they know best and have invested the most effort in. Therefore, the potential pitfall is relying on the quality of the product for creating a sustainable business. Owners following this plan don't replicate their business. Unless they progress past a product-focused mentality to a systems-focused mentality, they usually don't get much time away from the business. The owners following this path typically have a long road to profitability.

This kind of owner is the only type who might claim to close basically everyone they talk to. That is an indicator that they have more experience with membership sales with walk-ins, old clients, and referrals. They are rarely taking vacations. They often aren't spending enough time with their families. It's also usually difficult for them to manage more than one location well, because their business was built on their effort, not on systems that use the effort of others.

If you have ever encountered someone who's inclined to say, "We close everyone who comes in," don't assume that's a good thing. Dig a bit deeper. Ask questions to see what's going on under the surface. If the majority of their membership sales come from walk-ins and referrals, that's not a good sign. Ask if that owner is the one who's selling the memberships or if their team does the majority of the sales for them. Finally, find out what their life is like. Are they happy with the amount they work? Could they keep going forever at their current pace? Would other people be eager to live their life? If most of their sales come from organic sources, they probably do close most people that come in. However, they probably also do most of the work in their business themselves. As a result, their business might not be sustainable, and they likely do not have a scalable system.

Over-emphasizing the product in a sales environment is common to the Fitness Pro. Making too much of the business's daily operations reliant on the owner is the biggest and most common pitfall to this type.

What's great about the Fitness Pro is their ability to lead by example, their care for the quality of their product, and the passion they have for the success of their clients. You can always tell the difference between a gym owned by a real gym-head and one owned by someone who's not.

The most successful Fitness Pros emphasize recreating their strengths in others and building them up to manage daily operations of the business. They get out of the details of the day-to-day and focus on learning the areas of business and technology that they don't know. They do not obsess about becoming a master of those things, however. They learn enough to know how those things should run, then outsource them or train employees to handle those areas. They lead by example, vision, and inspiration.

The Franchisee

Franchisees are often in their forties to sixties. They have usually spent years as an employee and saved enough to invest in a business model. That model may or may not be able to reliably produce return on investment. Either way, there's less to learn and more support than opening an independent business, but less restriction and more potential upside than a job can provide.

They typically haven't spent years as a personal trainer or taught thousands of fitness classes because they have been primarily invested in a nine-to-five career. Fitness may be a business interest, personal hobby, or even a passion of theirs, but they usually aren't an industry expert when they invest in a franchise, otherwise they would have started an independent business on their own.

This background is beneficial because it has produced an investor's mindset from the start. They have more support with fewer decisions to make than the average Fitness Pro, but their investment in (and potential over-reliance on) a proven product can produce one of the biggest pitfalls for the Franchisee.

The franchisor sold the franchise to the Franchisee based on the value of their product. Then, the Franchisee absorbed that mentality and can overextend that outlook to the area of selling memberships. Not surprisingly, this perspective affects the way they handle their sales process—the quality of the product is why they bought the franchise, after all. The Franchisee then thinks that their members are like them and mostly interested in the quality of the product, so they start talking about how great their product is in order to make sales. That will work more often with the prospects who visit during the first few months of being open and less often as time goes on. Organic leads and founding members will join in spite of a poor sales process.

When that doesn't continue to work, they can be tempted to point the blame at the franchise. Restrictions imposed by the franchisor or feeling like the product is not as turnkey as the Franchisee wanted are common complaints. Those complaints are common to anyone in any franchise, but casting blame always leads to stagnation—and more blame casting. If a Franchisee is tempted to complain about the product, the focus shifts to changing the franchise instead of getting better at selling memberships.

The truth is that it's the job of the franchise to sell franchises and pool resources. It's the Franchisee's job to sell memberships and have a successful business. If that's you, remember the principle that comes from the section on ownership: No one is coming to save your business. The only person who's going to save your business is the one reading this book. If a person is to take full ownership of their business and life, they can't blame anyone else, no matter what. When that happens, personal growth is the only option. That's exactly where we all want to be, because growth is hard, but when it's the only option, it happens by default.

The average Franchisee has less of a challenge in front of them than the independent owner in some regards. There are fewer things to figure out and fewer chances for experimentation, which leaves fewer potential issues to grapple with. That's a great thing, because fewer options means more focus on what matters. Also, the added benefit of most franchises is that they will push an owner to open multiple locations. That's a benefit, because the owner is forced to have more of the daily business operations run by others, which is more likely to lead to freedom than trying to do everything yourself. Opening multiple locations is, in that sense, great for both the franchise and Franchisee. However, that can go very badly if a Franchisee isn't great at growing leaders for managing people and creating systems before they open additional locations. The worst pitfall is blaming the perpetually available target of the franchisor for anything that isn't great instead of focusing on things that can be controlled, but that pitfall is not unique to the Franchisee type. It is the fate of all humans who slip into passing blame instead of choosing to take action.

One of the great things about the Franchisee's mentality is that they are likely to bring new perspectives to the industry that come from their time in other industries. They are often eager to learn and grow, especially if they consider fitness to be a new industry for them. This mentality serves them well because that way of thinking is very valuable for the growth of any business. Leadership with pervasive lack of a desire for continued education—or resistance to being a "newbie"—is a death sentence. This is not the case for the Franchisee, as they are often reinventing themselves in taking on business ownership or exploring a new industry. They are also often inclined to outsource things they aren't an expert in, which is very useful—as long as they endure the learning curve of their first few bad hires and failed outsourcing attempts.

The Big Picture Thinker

The Big Picture Thinker sees the value of investing in the fitness industry, so they create their own product or invest in a franchise. It is often their intent to make it scalable and saleable from the start. The focus is for the business to run profitably without the owner's daily presence. The successful ones do not under-prioritize sales, retention, or referrals.

It doesn't matter if the Big Picture Thinker doesn't know how to lead a yoga practice, teach a spin class, or launch an advertisement. They know they can hire someone who knows how to do that. They seek to outsource everything they can to experts of that area. That leaves them the time to focus on building scalable systems that steer the business toward profitability. Profits happen quickly, or they don't happen at all and they move on. That frees this type to keep going until they do build something that's profitable.

The pitfalls are in spending money on things that don't matter to prospects or making wrong decisions about the features of their own product without regard to feedback from leads, their team and industry insiders. The most successful here act and adapt quickly, eagerly involve the blunt feedback of the market and industry insiders, and are good at instinctively ignoring non-crucial details.

The most likely to succeed in this category are the ones who hire well and have more than enough capital to invest. They hit the ground running, build scalable systems as they go, invest heavily in getting their first location to profitability, and repeat that process. They are playing to win with money they are prepared to lose. This enables them to make the fearless choices it takes to grow quickly and focus the majority of their energy on managing people well—or on the people they've hired who manage people well. This type will generally do well when they focus on finding people who can refine developing systems and execute effectively.

The Big Picture Thinker often isn't interested in doing anything on their own, so their ego is not in the way of hiring people who are better than they are at the particular task. They don't need to put in every last drop of the maximum possible effort to feel they've earned their success, but if they do, it's a sure path to burnout because their success should be outpacing their effort. The most effective of this class don't want to be the best at the daily operations, and that helps them to find or grow great leaders that surpass their own ability. The strength of their leaders who have been oriented for relentless focus on sales, retention, and referrals pulls the company forward into owning multiple locations. This is how the majority of the shining stars in business and any fitness franchise think.

There is a type of fitness business owner who doesn't start here, but becomes this Big Picture Thinker over time. They may have had small beginnings, but they are eager to learn and usually have an entrepreneurial bent, even if they had been using those skills to climb the corporate ladder. This type is categorized by their pursuit of growth and are motivated by the personal satisfaction of their own development and the development of others over other markers of success. They are not rigidly attached to a static perception of who they are and are willing to place themselves in new environments, even if it means being behind others of their own category. This gives them what it takes to become whatever they need to be. They act tenaciously and optimize for their own development and the growth of others. The growth of their business is the natural result.

Strategies of the most successful in all categories

Highly profitable fitness businesses are likely to have started driving leads and acquiring memberships before they were open. That's when there is no product. This keeps them from being able to overemphasize their product in the sales process. That takes care of the biggest and most common pitfall. It also forces strong sales skills right from the beginning.

Many experts become experts because they have been seeking growth habitually as a way of life. They don't usually think or say things like, "We already have it together and we close basically everyone." They are more prone to say, "We are always improving our sales skills." They are growth-hungry and their thought patterns are oriented toward areas of potential development, not where they feel they have already reached maximum development. This orientation produces habitual learning. Becoming an expert is the natural result. Once they become an expert, the habits that produced their expertise remain. That's why many of those who are great at things can sound like they are still learning. It's also why those not habitually seeking growth are rarely great.

In short, the most successful in all categories of owners are:

- Tenacious
- Great at hiring
- Habitually seek their own growth
- Not distracted by non-crucial details
- Focused on sales as the priority in all phases of a business
- Not spending their life on the daily operations of the business
- Intent on developing leaders and helping them surpass their own abilities

CHAPTER FIVE

The Buyer's Journey

*"I'm a success today because I had a friend who believed in me and
I didn't have the heart to let him down."*
- Abraham Lincoln

There are two types of leads in the world. Your business is equipped
for the first type and it *might* be ready for the second type. You may
find that your system has been unwittingly optimized for one type
over another. The two primary new lead sources are organic leads
and driven leads.

An organic lead is a prospect who finds your gym or studio and
comes in for a visit all on their own. An example of this is a guest
who comes in with a member or someone who finds your website or
phone number themselves and reaches out without any prompting
from you. A driven lead is a prospect whose interest was sparked
by some kind of offer you intentionally placed in their path with
marketing dollars. An example of this is a lead who provides their
contact information in response to paid advertising. Sometimes,
fitness business owners who have done incredibly well with organic
leads can fall flat on their face when they start working with driven
leads.

This is the realm of buyer psychology. In this world, prospects are
all the same, regardless of the product being sold. It is why people

produce the same objections to making a purchasing decision regardless of the product being sold or its price. Some of the more common ones sound like this: "I want to think about it," "I want to talk with my spouse [or business partner]," and, "It costs too much."

Most prospects we talk to from driven leads haven't made it far enough along their own thought process to realize all the reasons they are even interested in your facility. In order to address this we'll need to get a better understanding of these two types of leads. Organic leads are on the same path, but in a very different place.

The organic lead's journey

What actually causes an organic lead to join? For starters, the organic lead is likely to have spent months or years with the feeling of "going downhill" before showing up at your fitness business, while a driven lead is more likely to be brought in by a great offer and excellent follow up but would not have come in otherwise.

Let's imagine the first type of organic lead. This is the kind who shows up in your facility but does not currently work out. They have been feeling the pain of not being in the shape they'd like to be in. This is the state in which they remain until something changes. They start with some research and locate some facilities in their area. That may be where the journey starts and ends for some. In the context of lifestyle and habits, for that person to show up in a gym, the friction of remaining the same has to become greater than the friction of leaving the safety of their current patterns behind.

For the organic lead to arrive at your facility, the first of a series of hurdles to overcome is the fear of being the "new guy" and potential judgment. Charging down a path that includes the risk of not being accepted raises red flags. This happens on deep levels that are capable of triggering anxiety to the point that it can be measured by *physical* symptoms. The potential of being judged and found unworthy is enough to freeze many into inaction.

In order to avoid the intensity of those red flags, an organic lead often tries working out on their own instead of going to a gym. They'll dust off the rusty gym equipment in their basement one more time or eat a salad here and there, but the type who are most likely to make it to your gym will not do that often enough to see great results or consistent progress. So, when a prospect does come in and says, "I work out at home," it's a great bet their home workouts aren't working.

Eventually, the false starts of the home workout and unsustainable dieting can cause an organic lead to become unwilling to continue to accept their current patterns. For many of those who do show up, there has been some process of internal development before external changes begin. You'll primarily see the very brave, the highly pained, or the ones who have become free from the pursuit of acceptance. The important thing to note about this type is this: before showing up, something *internal* has changed for them. Something within them gave way as they expanded internally. They have shed a shell and hit a new state of internal strength before anything in their external world shifted.

That kind of organic lead will arrive at your facility free, confident, and exhilarated. They will be walking in newfound success before coming in. They will be equipped with the mental determination to push through. They've already made it through various types of barriers on the long path to your facility. They arrive in your parking lot knowing exactly what lies behind them is what lies in their future if they don't do something different than what they have been doing. They walk in, take a class, and sign on the dotted line. This type of lead will sign up regardless of the sales process in place.

An analogy from one of my most influential mentors in the fitness industry comes to mind: these new members are like a brave dog who has overcome the fear of the electric fence. First, they pressed on through the anguish of anticipating pain. Second, they physically blasted through the actual pain of the invisible fence (one of our workouts). Third, after finding they haven't died, are rewarded by the exhilarating freedom of the other side. With this newfound momentum, the next fence will have to be much stronger to slow their progress. Yet somehow we think they joined because the hard work we provided them with was so great!

This same concept applies to member retention. They developed strength to not only join but to attend your fitness facility long term *before* coming in. After six months, they are not an outsider. Instead, they have become part of a like-minded community. After a year, they are proud of how far they've come and start inviting the friends who have noticed how they've changed. Those friends come in and are easily integrated into the group so they all live happily ever after.

The second type of organic lead is the one who already works out. Generally, they find a facility and join on their own. They do that because some change, like moving or changing jobs, causes them to seek a new facility. There's no invisible electric fence to overcome because they've already done that long ago.

The third type of organic lead is a referral of a member. Referrals fall into two categories, which makes them tricky if you're not paying attention. One type of referral comes in because they are *internally* motivated themselves. In that case, the referring member just smooths the path to your fitness facility. That type of referral will mostly join on their own, just like any other organic lead. The other type of referral is *externally* motivated. That's what happens when the member referring the lead is pushing them in. In that case, there will be a lot more work to do on our part. The following discussion of leads driven by marketing and follow up will readily apply to this type of referral.

The driven lead's journey

Let's take a look at the driven lead. At just the right moment, they notice an advertisement for a local fitness facility. The offering is tantalizing enough for them to want to learn more. They take the bait, often thinking, "Eh, why not? I should do something about this at some point." They share inaccurate contact information or an old email address, not wanting to be bombarded by follow up. Now, the driven lead's conscience is satisfied with the thought of doing something at some point. The anchorless, "I'll do something, someday, sometime," thinking drifts off into the distance. The end.

This is the level where many driven leads originate and die for all but the most adept marketers. The acquisition of a "lead" is made, but rarely results in a membership. This is what happens with most marketing that doesn't come with good follow up. Just think about billboards on the side of the highway. How often do you take new action as a result of seeing a billboard? Probably not very often. How often do you even *notice* billboards?

So let's say a gym owner, Greg, knows all this, and hires an experienced, expensive marketer to get leads. This marketer spends his days and nights obsessing over getting the leads to not only express interest but also to share *good* contact information. That contact information is then sent to Greg.

The next morning when Greg starts working, he finds a pleasant surprise. "How exciting! A lead!" Greg sends the lead a message saying, "When would you like to come by?" He does this using exactly what has always worked for the organic leads. Greg leans back, smiles, and waits expectantly. A day goes by with no response.

Greg thinks to himself, "I don't want to sound pushy or desperate. I'll send a reminder message tomorrow."

The reminder message goes out, and a few more days go by. No response. After a week, Greg realizes that this lead probably isn't going to respond. In desperation, Greg picks up the phone to call the lead. No answer. Greg leaves a message, trying to sound positive, motivating, and exciting but still including a tiny little jab of guilt. Just something to push the lead into action.

Ultimately, Greg gets tired of trying to get the lead to answer and writes them off as a bad lead. "They must not have really been that interested in the first place." This pattern repeats itself for a few weeks. Greg begins to think his marketer must be targeting the wrong kinds of leads. That's the *only* logical conclusion Greg can think of.

This is the second level, where this group of driven leads from high-paid, expert marketers die. In the opinion of the marketer, they have provided leads. Their job is done. In the opinion of the owner, the goal of membership growth has been totally missed. The problem is this: neither the marketer or the owner realize that driven leads start to fade within seconds of not being contacted. The marketer receives pressure to improve the lead quality, but lead quality is not the problem.

Now, let's imagine a third scenario where the expert marketing is aided with excellent lead nurturing. This time, instead of the lead being left to rot and die on the vine, the lead gets an immediate message. The message is not just any willy nilly combo of letters. No, this verbiage has been perfected over hundreds of thousands of leads. This causes a new lead to book an appointment right then and there from their couch. All this happens within seconds, before anything else can pull on the driven lead's attention and money.

Gym Membership Sales

A day later, the lead receives a text message reminding them of their upcoming workout. The reminder uses the exact words that are most likely to cause the lead to show up. They show up, try the workout, and love it.

It's the exact same great workout that all the current members and organic leads get. Now, the moment of truth approaches. Greg presents all membership options. It's on a sliding price scale based on length of commitment with a few other options based on frequency of use. The owner even throws in the class-pack options for good measure. That way, there's for sure something that fits exactly what the lead wants. The owner makes a recommendation to choose the twelve-month commitment option. Everything goes exactly as it would be to all the organic leads. The driven lead shifts his feet, adjusting his position.

He takes a deep breath, clears his throat and says, "I love it here, thanks so much for the workout. I'm definitely going to join!"

"Great!" The owner shoots back, "Which membership do you want?"

The lead hesitates and says, "Well… I just want to think about it for a day or two." Then, seeing the owner's dismay, the lead throws in, "I'll also see if my wife wants to come too, that way maybe we can both join."

Great, Greg thinks, *I've invested a ton of money in getting these leads. They'll be back for sure.*

So Greg waits for this lead and all the other driven leads to act like organic leads. A few days go by and Greg sends a series of messages, then a call. As the weeks go by, the lead gets a voicemail and another series of messages. Do you want to know what happens next? Absolutely nothing. Greg never sees this driven lead (or his wife) ever again and decides it must have been another bad lead.

This little story is more common than it should be. I have talked with hundreds of other gym owners who were stuck, even though some of them had received thousands of leads. If you speak to enough people, you'll hear a version of this same story over and over, too.

So how can we fix what's going on here? Why do the driven leads fail to make it across the finish line and buy a membership in a facility where the organic leads show up and join all the time? Why do driven leads even interact with the advertising to begin with if they aren't actually going to join?!

Owners with this problem often have a sense that something is wrong but can't put their finger on it. It can lead to flailing from one lead generation tool to the next and giving up, or making an inch of progress in one hundred different directions but never finding the source of the issue.

Same path, different journey

Grasping and fixing the problem of "bad leads" comes down to the concept I call the "buyer's journey." The organic lead is likely to have been on the buyer's journey for months, years, or even decades. Many of them are already pursuing a fitness lifestyle. The point of driving leads is to accelerate that process. What took an organic lead years of development to "level up" internally before arriving does not occur in the case of many driven leads. The truth is that "bad leads" are not on a different path than "good leads." They are on the same path, just in different places.

The driven lead did not reach out or come in on their own. That's the tiny difference with big underlying implications. The driven lead needed the offer from the marketing, often with multiple impressions, plus the support of razor-sharp lead nurturing to actually show up in the facility. The organic lead needed none of that. The driven leads often do not have that same internal strength or intent that the organic leads do (yet). If they did, they would have already overcome any hurdles and joined somewhere on their own. There's less motivation for the average driven lead compared to the average organic lead because of where they are on the buyer's journey.

The difference in organic leads and driven leads is the reason some owners have actually come across great lead sources and discarded them. If an owner treats driven leads like organic leads, the driven leads will rarely join. It's like owning a gasoline-powered car and putting diesel in it.

If there are problems with driven leads, do not jump to the conclusion that the leads are bad. The first thing to do is to identify whether the problem is that the leads aren't coming in, or rather that they *are* coming in but aren't joining. Then go deeper. If they aren't coming in, is it primarily because they aren't booking appointments? Or is it because they aren't showing up for the appointments they book? Keep asking questions like this until you locate the root of the primary issue. Then work on whatever the root is.

All that makes sense, but it's still difficult to perfect the process. Most people don't have the time or money to follow up with thousands of leads until appointment booking systems are razor sharp. The next curve is getting people to show up for those appointments. After that, the process becomes perfecting the close ratio of that type of lead. Then retaining them, and then acquiring maximum referrals. Doing all of that is tough. In a real-life moment, it can *seem* like it would be easier to simply switch to a "better" source of leads. The problem with that is switching vendors every few months isn't without its costs, either. It's also important to note that unsuccessful people do not habitually invest in finding the root of the problem. On so many levels, duct taping the bumper cover on a car is easier than adjusting a bent frame so that the bumper cover fits properly. There are costs to either path, so be sure you choose intentionally.

People who invest in moving away from doing most of the tasks in their business to make time to work on the processes like these are the ones who get to spend time growing their businesses. If that's where you're headed, the list below will help you identify bottlenecks in this area. Here are some potential indicators of a sales process that's likely to be distorted by organic leads:

- The primary people responsible for membership sales are inclined to talk as if they close every sale.
- There isn't a significant focus in ongoing sales training.
- The majority of the leads are organic or referrals from organically generated memberships.
- The owner is the primary person selling the memberships.
- If the owner tried to open a second facility or take a vacation, their first facility would struggle.
- The owner doesn't have a sustainable and enjoyable work/life balance because they do not own a business that runs without them.

The more of the above points are true, the more likely it is for problems to exist. Not having enough revenue to afford to outsource other tasks in the business leaves the owner teaching the classes, handling the bookkeeping, cleaning, posting on social media, doing the sales, getting in early, and staying late to keep up with everything. That doesn't leave time for refining systems and will not produce a scalable business, because the systems being developed are not being created to run without the owner. If that sounds like it could be you, don't worry. Identifying precisely where you are, even when it hurts, is the first step of progress.

The Solution

The realization that organic leads and driven leads are on the exact same path, just in different places, is the key to creating membership acquisition systems that work for all leads, regardless of where they are along the spectrum. Driven leads clicked on the ad in the first place because they are on the buyer's journey—albeit, very early in the journey. If the marketing and lead nurturing accomplish their jobs, driven leads have had that process shortened. So, many times, the better the marketing and lead nurturing, the earlier the leads will be captured on their journey. Because of the current volume of marketing outreach and its increasing effectiveness, time on the buyer's journey before lead acquisition is shorter. So, the development of leads is far less than it ever was in the past. Does anyone remember when print ads, banners and handing out guest passes actually worked as a viable marketing strategy? Has anyone noticed that those things almost never work anymore? Except for in very rare circumstances and odd pockets, leads are captured so early on their journey by the effectiveness of modern marketing and lead nurturing. This works so well that old marketing measures can't keep up.

As the strength of marketing and lead nurturing increases, our strength in sales training must follow. Many of our leads will not be as far along the buyer's journey as they were in years prior. That doesn't change the fact that we believe in their ability to succeed. Installing a system in your business that reliably produces progression along the buyer's journey and success for your prospects is what we're getting into next.

CHAPTER SIX

Four Segment Sales System - Needs Assessment

"'Discipline equals freedom' applies to every aspect of life: if you want more freedom, get more discipline."
– Jocko Willink

This segment is about taking a closer look at practical tools that apply to our industry. Remember, these practical tools will only be useful in the long term if they're built on good foundations. Too often people see the fruit—like money, a great relationship, or a high close ratio—and want to jump right to the result without growing the underlying roots. As we progress, remember to keep the cultivation of your mentality as the priority. With the right mental habits and subsequent supporting culture, great results from practical tools will be natural. This is not about selling a product; it's about teaching your team to bring people to a decision. We do this with the intent to change lives, not make sales. Don't worry—increased revenue *will* be the result.

Those less experienced in sales might be tempted to think their unique unicorn of a product dictates a unique sales system. The reason it doesn't is simple: at a foundational level, sales processes aren't built on the product—they're built on how humans think.

People's reasons for taking any action or buying anything are all exactly the same on core levels.

Hear me out: We're not trying to become better at closing membership sales based on the merits of our product. This is a selfish view of the world and doesn't work well in sales. Instead, we're improving our ability to help a person arrive at a decision based on *their* needs and wants. It's not about us or our cool product. No matter how great the thing is we're selling, what matters most are the needs and core drivers of the people we serve. This shift in focus is what increases close ratios, retention, and referrals. Those foundational elements are what the following sales process is built on.

Overview of the Four-Segment Sales System

The framework I'll be sharing with you here can be applied to any sales environment, because buyer psychology is the same in any environment. However, the details of the terminology will vary. What's written here is optimized for a fitness membership sale.

Keep in mind that this is *not* designed to produce a "yes" from a prospect at all costs. It's made to get a prospect out of the gray space of "maybe" and into a "yes" or "no" decision. This is also *not* designed for selling to people who should not purchase a fitness membership from you. That is rare because it is an odd person who goes out of their way to visit a gym or studio that they have zero need of with no interest in health and fitness. This process is also *not* made for the other extreme: someone who's just going to sign up for a membership on their own with no sales process whatsoever. This is usually 10–15 percent of the prospects that are produced by marketing. (Side note: if you're closing 15 percent or less of your prospects that come in from marketing efforts, this means you have little to no sales process or a very broken one and this is especially for you, so press on.)

This process *is* made for the largest segment of the population. Seventy percent or so of prospects are the middle of the standard deviation curve. These are the people who *should* invest in their heath and fitness and *will* purchase a membership and use it, but *only* with the right onboarding process. On a practical level, your team needs to know that helping this category of the population is where we can make the biggest difference in the world. It is also where the biggest opportunity lies for our gyms. Helping that sort of person, the one who needs our help but will only get it with the right onboarding process, is the exact person this sales system is intended for.

One final caveat before we start: be sure to teach and implement the Four Segment Sales System in your business, segment by segment. Implementing this process and training your team one segment at a time is much easier than working on everything at once. Do not force yourself or your team to try to focus on all four segments at once. That's a sure recipe for failure. Instead, focus on one segment at a time in implementation and in ongoing training. What you'll find is that improving closing ratios is just like eating an elephant: the only way to do it is one bite at a time.

Here's an overview of the whole process:

Segment One: Needs Assessment. This is where we'll spend the majority of our time to draw out what a prospect wants. I'll give you questions to use and ways of practicing before using these things with a real prospect. When this is done well, we build a strong foundation for a change to occur in someone's life. We will also go over how to approach objections before they arise, before presenting price.

Segment Two: Price Packaging and Presentation Secrets. This is where I'll show you a price presentation style that will help make it easier for prospects to make a decision. It's also an effective way to have employees make more sales without you being there, because membership will be offered in the same compelling way, every time.

Segment Three: Embracing Objections. This is where I'll give you a simple outline for what to do with all of the most common objections. You've heard objections like, "I want to think about it," "I want to talk with my husband/wife about it," and, "It costs too much," before. We'll talk about how to prevent them from ever occurring in the first place.

Segment Four: Onboarding and Retention. This is where I'll share some simple tools to increase retention and new member referrals. You'll want immediate referrals from brand-new members as well as ongoing referrals. Immediate referrals are the most valuable because it helps new members stay longer and get what they came for. This is the easiest way to get more bang for your buck.

The Four Segment Sales system is designed for you to influence your average member's investment over the life of their membership so that more prospects join, more lives are changed, and more revenue growth happens on purpose.

Segment One: Needs Assessment

The first and most important segment of a great sales process is the needs assessment. This is the phase where we seek to draw out detailed information from the prospect in the following areas:

- Where they are now
- Where they want to be
- What achieving that will do for them
- What has kept them from achieving this already

The majority of the answers to these things will seem obvious. Much of the information can be guessed correctly within a minute or less. Regardless, we want to train our teams to invite the prospect to describe these areas in detail for two main reasons:

1. Just because an observer of someone's life can see that someone needs something, doesn't mean the person being observed can.
2. The goal is to align the prospect and salesperson. Even if the observations are obvious, speaking them out loud causes both the salesperson and prospect to feel what's *associated with* the observations.

Remember, logical facts do not produce action—emotions do. That's why we're focusing on drawing out their story. When a prospect describes the details of their optimal future, emotions will rise to the surface. We are not, regardless of what we'd like to believe, rational beings. Action is either initiated by or impeded by emotions. It's supported with logic, but created by emotion.

As aforementioned, drawing out someone's story takes an open and inviting mental posture free of judgment on the part of the salesperson or it won't work. I call this state "clean slate curiosity." When we train our teams to approach a prospect with zero assumptions and to ask good questions, the prospect shares easily. When they share easily, it's easier to do their needs assessment well. When their needs assessment is done well, the majority of the sale handles itself. Even if objections arise, we'll have all the ammunition needed to help a prospect progress past their own fear-based barriers.

The easiest way for us to teach a sales team to do this consistently is by practicing with a script. There are a few people who may be blindly resistant to the concept of a script, especially the more experienced, free-spirited types like me, because they see scripts as limiting their creativity or making the experience feel artificial. But a script is only a pathway for doing something in a consistent fashion until you develop the natural habit the script leads to. Many elite sales experts use scripts because it keeps them on a regular path without needing to think about it. That leaves no energy expended on what's coming next in the conversation, enabling salespeople to focus all their brain energy on listening to their prospect.

The customized scripts you'll develop here might only be used for training purposes, or it might be the exact, word-for-word phrases to use for a real sales conversation. The important thing isn't the use of the script, but the changing of more lives. I've helped lots of fitness businesses quadruple their close ratio by giving them sales scripts.

Owners will benefit exponentially by making the process of membership sales a clear pathway that's done the same way each time. The fewer chances to deviate, the better. The fewer decisions to make on the part of the salesperson, the better. A fine-tuned pathway to long-term membership that's repeated consistently is our goal.

Segment One: How the Needs Assessment should sound

If a prospect walks out saying they need to "think about it" before making a decision, it's probably exactly why they have a reason to show up in the first place. They probably won't come back, and your chance for changing a life will have been blown, because when they leave, they will have less support in overcoming their old thoughts than they do with you. They will stagnate.

We're looking to do two things in the needs assessment:

1. Dissolve objections to making a decision
2. Unearth the prospect's core drivers

Remember, modern marketing and follow-up is so powerful that we encounter a high percentage of prospects that are in the first steps of the buyer's journey. Sometimes, our prospects haven't fully acknowledged what's motivating them. They haven't paused to assess the far-reaching effects of change they are considering. By asking questions around these topics, we're helping prospects discover and solidify their reasons for overcoming the pain of change.

As we do that, we'll be discovering their core drivers. This produces the potent combination of emotions to initiate action, as well as the logic to support the choice. This brief moment of clarity can still be met with objections, but the steps for bringing someone to a decision can be surprisingly systematic. We're looking to bring logic and emotion into harmony, then to provide a safe space for a choice.

Ultimately, sales is a creative endeavor. We're not trying to change that. We're just looking to eliminate as many variables as possible. The strength of creativity comes with the responsibility to develop focus. What we're doing in training is making it easy for a salesperson to focus their creativity.

That's why the needs assessment and objectionhandling processes should be drilled with a script in hand, especially in the beginning, until it's part of the sales team's unconscious pattern. We want them to naturally unearth a prospect's current situation, their goals, how the achievement of those goals will have a broader impact on their lives, what the barriers to success have been, and how important forward progress is to the prospect. The scripting is just the outline to a salesperson's creative energy along a proven path. Once that pattern is second-nature, the salesperson gets to focus the majority of their energy on listening. This results in more focus on what a prospect is not saying, which in turn makes it much easier to see what the prospect's objections are likely to be.

Upon noticing a likely objection during the Needs Assessment, the well-trained salesperson then asks questions around that topic, with the intent to draw out that hesitation before presenting the price of membership. This can be planned for as well, because we already know what most objections are likely to be. Keep in mind that objections aren't resistance to the product. For most people, objections are resistance to making a decision or, on deeper levels, incongruent feelings around the achievement of their own goals.

The majority of the objections will fit within two categories:

1. Delay of decision
   o "I just want to think about it"
   o "I'll join when ___ happens"
   o "I want to talk with my significant other about it"

2. Value:
   o "It costs too much"
   o "I'm paying less than that at ___"
   o "I'm not sure I'll have enough time"
   o "The class times don't work very well for me; if you offered something at ___, I'd join"
   o "I'm afraid that I'll pay for it and get no results"

These aren't objections to your membership. They are the same excuses all human brains use when resisting any decision. Everyone in sales and marketing deals with these same hangups, no matter the industry.

Knowing this means that with just a little listening, we can easily identify the likely objections of each prospect and address them before presenting price. Your mission in practicing and coaching a script will be to build this habit.

For instance, when you recognize that someone hasn't been spending any money on fitness or has only invested in cheap options in the past, you can probably guess that one of their objections, regardless of how much money they have, is likely to be about the expense. This is what some people call a "price objection," but the real reason for this price objection is not the cost—it's the cost of investment in comparison to the value. Upon recognizing this during your needs assessment, you'll ask questions that will help establish the actual value of the membership in the prospect's life. That's done with questions like these:

- What would it be like if you were to invest in a higher-quality program than the membership you currently have?
- If you were investing in a premium experience, do you think you might be more likely to use it?
- Do you think you might enjoy a nice facility more than a cheap one? Do you think that might help you?
- If you were to use a facility like this pretty regularly for six months or so, what sorts of things do you think you might achieve? How would that impact your life? Would that do anything for anyone besides you? How would that impact your career and finances? And for you, which of these things matters most to you? How important is that?

And so on, in order to address the price objection in their old thought patterns before presenting price. If someone establishes the value of the return on investment in their own life based on playing out the implications of the changes that would come from regularly using a gym membership, you're much less likely to encounter a value objection. In this way, the new client makes the sale themselves based on the implications of what the membership is likely to help them with in their life. However, if a price or value objection does still manage to hang on through that process and surface later on with a prospect saying something like, "It all sounds great, but I just have to check on my finances," you'll be equipped with information that will help the prospect get out of the gray space and to a decision.

That will sound something like this, "Okay, if this doesn't work for your spending plan, that's totally okay. Other than the finances, does everything else look good? Okay, great. And earlier you said that working out in a facility like this would help you achieve ____ (insert whatever their most important lifestyle impact was from the questions above). Is that still very important to you?" They'll have to admit that it's true. Then, you'll respond with, "Great, then let's get you started."

At this point, they will agree with your support in helping them reach the things they came there for that are much more important than money, and they will sign up. Or, the real objection will surface, and you'll be a big step closer to their "yes" or "no" decision.

Similarly, knowing that "I need to think about it," is a likely objection for anyone, we can prepare for it and address it before it comes out in a statement like that. This objection usually comes from fear of the unknown in one way or another. Fear of the unknown is normal and common because it nearly always feels safer to remain the same than it does to try something new and different, regardless of reality. This fear preventing someone from making a "yes" or "no" decision about a membership is often rooted in one or both of these areas:

1. Not helping your prospect consider and decide about the smaller aspects of your solution along the way before

inviting them to consider the ultimate decision of whether or not your solution is right for them.

2. Old habits of hesitating on the brink of healthy change.

To prevent the objection of "I need to think about it," ask questions around these topics before presenting the membership investment. The questions that prevent this objection due to not considering the smaller choices along the way will sound like this:

- Do you like it here?
- Is this location convenient for you?
- What do you think you might get here that you aren't getting out of what you're currently doing for your health and fitness?
- What days and times do you think you might come by if you were to train here? Okay, now that we've figured that out, would that work with the rest of your schedule?

The questions that prevent the "I want to think about it" objection due to normal hesitancy on the brink of a change will sound like this:

- How long ago did you start noticing that it might be nice to ____ (fill in that blank with the prospect's reason for coming in. "Tone up," for example)? Okay, and how long have you been thinking about doing something about that?
- How long has it been since you've had a fitness routine that was helping you achieve those goals?
- Why not just keep doing what you were doing before you visited here?
- How long have you been thinking about making a change to a different style of fitness? What do you think it would be like if you did?

- What other areas of your life would that impact?
- How important is that to you?

Our intent is to help a prospect replace any old patterns of thinking by moving past them into actually changing. When we clear those old patterns out of the way and treat them as things that have served our prospect in the past, but no longer do, the sale takes care of itself. If, however, this objection still happens to appear after presenting the price of membership, you'll be equipped to address it by saying things like, "Okay, take all the time you need to think about it, but what is it you need to think about?" Then, the real objection is likely to surface. If that truly is the objection, you will find yourself equipped and ready to say something like, "Okay. Other than spending some time thinking about it, does everything else look good? Okay, great, and earlier you said you've been thinking about getting in better shape for the last few years and that you can't keep doing what you had been doing before you came in here because ___ (fill this blank in with their words). Is it in your best interest to keep thinking about it? It isn't? Okay, let's go ahead and get you started!"

Similarly to the other basic and typical objections above, we know people are likely to say "I want to talk with my partner about it" rather than making a decision. So, we're going to discover if that objection is their reality or just a desire to avoid making a choice by asking questions like:

- Does your partner like to ___ (insert your genre of fitness here: work out, practice yoga, cycle, etc.) as well?
- Is your significant other supportive, neutral, or against you making progress in this area?
- What would your partner say if you were to make progress on the path to achieving ___?

Most often, but not always, the answers to these questions will reveal that their partner is supportive. If they say the partner is supportive, we'll follow it up with a question like, "Your partner is supportive?" or, "Okay, tell me more about that." This will give your prospect space to describe that in more detail. We're seeking to draw out and solidify the likely response that their partner would be happy for them to invest in their own health and fitness. (If you're one of the few who are worried about asking questions like this, get over it quickly. When you are worried about upsetting someone, it will taint all of your communication. Our own anxiety or worry can cause questions to sound very serious and seem like they carry a lot of weight. When you aren't worried about upsetting anyone as a habit, you'll be more likely to communicate in a fun, casual way that puts others at ease.) Ask questions like these, combined with well-timed pauses to allow the prospect's reality to sink in. Take your time along the buyer's journey and allow your prospect's thoughts to assimilate.

If you have already learned about a prospect's supportive partner and then, after presenting the price of membership, the prospect still says, "I need to talk with my partner about it first," you are well armed to handle it. That might sound something like this: "Sure, take all the time you need to talk it over... Earlier you said that your partner has been pushing you to take better care of yourself. It sounds to me like they will like this, won't they?" They'll have to admit that it's true. Then, you'll respond with, "Great, then let's get you started."

Many objections are just born of the normal human desire to remain the same, rather than make a decision or take on the risk of something new or different. Another one of my favorite objections to practice with a team is the objection related to the prospect's perceived shortage of time. It sounds like: "I'm just not sure that

I have enough time to use it," or, "I just don't know if I'll have enough time to come in often enough to get my money's worth." It's a funny objection, and setting someone free from this mentality has powerful implications across their life.

When a prospect says, "I don't have enough time," it comes from a state of mind that is only a distraction, obscuring the decision at hand. As we all know, having enough time is really just a matter of priorities. So if a person is experiencing the feeling that they might not have enough time, our job is to invite that person away from the distraction of that feeling and toward choosing to invest their time in alignment with where they'd like to go. Often, people who present this objection feel at the mercy of the business of life. Our job is to invite people into an ownership role instead of a victim mentality by helping them arrive at the conclusion that they have the ability to choose where their time goes.

Struggling to make enough time to produce a desired change comes from having habits that no longer support where someone wants to go. We can see this "time" objection as a prospect reaching out for help with their priorities, if indeed making a change toward a healthier lifestyle is truly their intent. The way to address a time objection is just like any other. It's easiest to address early, and we do so by drawing out the value of the inevitable time tradeoff before presenting the price of membership. In this way, you can see how the "I'm not sure I have enough time" objection actually fits under the category of a value objection. Knowing this, you can ask questions around value and priorities to head the "time" objection off before presenting price. Remember that the value to a prospect is found in the implications of the achievements, not the achievements themselves. Once that value is drawn out, then priorities can be established.

Questions like this in the needs assessment will help:

- If you were to prioritize using a facility like this for the next few months, what do you think you might achieve?
- Would you have more energy? Is it possible that this would help you be more efficient in other areas of life? Tell me more about that.
- Why not just continue on your current path at your current pace without making time for fitness?
- Do you think something like using this studio might help you manage your average week more efficiently? What would that do for you? How would that impact the other parts of your life?
- So for you, is this worth focusing on? How long do you think it might take for you to start feeling the benefits of using a facility like this?
- When you have chosen to allocate time to working out and you achieve [prospect's goal], how would that feel? How important is that to you?

Then, if you still encounter an objection related to shortage of time when presenting the price of membership, you'll be ready. If someone says, "I like it here, but I'm just not sure that I have enough time to use the membership," you'll be able to say something like this: "If making time in your schedule for this isn't a good fit, that's totally okay. Earlier you said that it's very important for you to achieve ____ because of ____. Is that still true? Great, let's go ahead and get you started."

This will help you bring someone to a clear "Yes, I'm in" or "No, I'm not" decision based on what matters most to them. Remember, any decision is a good decision. Anything that's in the gray space of "likely," "maybe," "possibly," or "potentially" is what we cannot accept. In sales, hearing a clear yes or no at the end of each conversation, with either response being a success, is the standard to uphold.

Hearing, "I'll join later on" as an objection to starting a fitness membership today can be confusing. This is tricky, because the drive to hesitate on the brink of a choice can cause a prospect to fool themselves and you into fully believing that they'll be coming back to join another day. However, if they say "tomorrow I'll join," it's probably exactly what they've been saying for months. When tomorrow arrives, it's exactly what they'll say then, too. Believing this to be true is like having the ability to see into the future by observing the past.

Lives are not changed when we leave prospects in the gray "maybe" space. When a prospect doesn't make a choice as a result of our conversation with them, we leave them in the same, actionless holding pattern they were in before our conversation with them. But if we bring a prospective member to a place of clarity where they can make a clear choice of "yes" or "no" about our solution to their situation, they can put their effort into making progress on what they came there for in the first place, or put their effort into finding the right solution for their situation.

Accept no gray space. Do not allow your own decisions or others' decisions to linger when you're given the opportunity to help them find clarity. Set your intention to bring all your prospects to a clear "yes" or "no" today. If they can't make a choice today with your support, they won't stand a chance without you.

To do any of this well, it's important to understand that prospects aren't actually interested in achieving their goals. They are actually interested in the implications of the achievements and how those implications impact their lives. The *feelings* that the achievement of the goals will bring is what produces the motivation to push past the fear of the unknown and into making a choice. Painting a verbal picture of the lifestyle impacts they are looking for (and experiencing the feelings that will come with that expression) helps a person prioritize the achievement of the goals. Imagining a better scenario produces hope and creates an opportunity for that possibility in someone's life that might not exist otherwise. Hope is a powerful drug, and a little pile of emotions are more powerful for producing change than whole stacks of logic.

So, instead of selling the workouts or goals, focus on learning what someone wants and find out how it will feel to them when they realize the implications of what they want to achieve. When you do this well, your membership is only the vehicle to move a person in the direction they'd like to go.

Remember, objections are normal human responses that happen when people are on the verge of making a decision. Plan for and train for objections so your team will be ready to dissolve them before presenting the price of membership. You'll find more practical tools for putting these concepts into action in the online resources. You're now equipped to see the likely future for your team and your prospects. Start preparing to influence it.

Script elements and follow-up questions

You can use these principles to create your own questions and produce a script tailored to your company for training and practice purposes. The script shouldn't be written for you and your team to follow step by step. Think of it more like producing guidelines for your team by outlining the bullet points of the ideal conversation. This will make it easier to practice and prepare for speaking with prospects, dissolving their common objections, and helping them come to a clear decision. Don't waste time practicing for objections you rarely hear; only focus on what your team is very likely to encounter and ignore the rest.

Use the following topics to guide your company's unique script:

- What does the prospect's life look like now?
- Where do they want to be?
- What will achieving that do for them?
- What has kept them from achieving this already?
- How important is the achievement of these things to them?

There should also be three to five follow-up questions under each topic that flow out of the conversation. As a general rule, follow-up questions happen after the sales person asks a question about a main topic. This is because the "gold" of that topic is often three to five questions below the surface level of that topic.

Here's how it might go: Imagine your salesperson has just encountered a prospect and asks, "What are you doing for your workouts now?"

Prospect: I'm working out at home.

Your salesperson (this is where follow-up questions for this topic start):

- Working out at home (mirroring the significant words from their last statement)?
- How's that going for you?
- How long has it been like that?
- What makes you say that?
- Why is that important to you?
- How does that impact your life?
- Is that affecting any other areas of your life?

- What would it be like if you were to ___ for a few months?
- How do you think that might impact your life going forward?
- Tell me more about that.

Without a few of those follow-up questions, the prospect's original statement of "I'm working out from home" doesn't provide much clarity to them or insight to the salesperson. But you can imagine that, after a few of the questions above, the gold from several layers below the prospect's initial reply is likely to be discovered.

This script or ideal conversation outline continues in the online resources that accompany this book. Feel free to make adaptations to it based on the principles from this segment. If you'd like a template of this entire conversation, access the online resources now found at www.membershipsalesbook.com/resources.

CHAPTER SEVEN

Four Segment Sales System - Packaging and Presentation

"The way to create something great is to create something simple."
– Richard Koch, The 80/20 Principle: The Secret to Achieving More with Less

There are many ways that members pay to use a fitness facility:

- Month-to-month unlimited
- Twelve month commitment, unlimited use
- Once, twice, or three times per week, month to month
- Once, twice, or three times per week, twelve-month commitment
- Single day pass
- Guest pass for a friend
- Four, eight, twelve, or twenty pack
- One week, two week, or one month unlimited pass
- Three, six, or twelve months paid in full

That doesn't even include any of the fancier onboarding tools like:

- Fast-action incentives
- Low barrier entry offers
- Starting with short-term challenges then upgrading prospects to membership

- Long ramping up or on-boarding processes that require a higher investment for the first few weeks
- Enrollment fees
- Annual fees
- Founding member specials
- New Year's specials
- Black Friday deals

And that's just a sampling... How many possible combinations could be produced? Is your head spinning with all the possibilities? Just imagine what it's like for the team that has to pitch some combination of those membership options and incentives to prospects. Even worse, think of the prospect who's already stressed out by being somewhere new. They are already wrestling natural internal conflicts over the consideration of a lifestyle change. Is it really a good idea for us to ask them to choose between five or six membership options?

Lots of owners try a pricing sheet to make the options clear, in plain black and white for everyone. This can help a prospect make sense of the options and prevent the team from having to memorize them, but a clearer look at complexity is still just a better look at something that's complex. Put plainly, an organized, laminated turd is still a turd.

Too many ways of paying for membership or class packs is a sign that the designer of the price packaging is trying to give all potential new members whatever they want instead of selling people what they need—like a change of lifestyle. Presenting three or fewer ways of paying for workouts is an easy way to increase the volume of revenue in a fitness business without having to increase the volume of prospects. Let me explain.

Class packs

Non-recurring class packages are very far from memberships. Retention is challenging enough without building attrition into our packaging. Yes, it feels nice to make a sale, but it is at the expense of the opportunity to create a recurring sale.

I've talked with studios who have thousands of "members" who were just people with class passes left on their punch cards. By the monthly volume of prospects and the sizes of their databases, everything looks great. Their revenue, however, is suffering. For example, just two hundred members at typical studio rates of $135–$185 per month bring in $27,000–$37,000 per month, and that recurs automatically. Two hundred members is way better than a thousand class pass holders who paid a flat rate once and may never spend money at your facility again. Amazon doesn't sell a twelve-month Prime membership that just ends; it recurs automatically for a reason. Notice: with fewer price options that are packaged well, the prospect volume can remain the same, the number of sales can go down, and yet the volume of revenue can drastically increase.

In this case, less is more:

- More income with fewer sales
- More real members with fewer options
- More sales with less effort spent explaining options
- More prospect decisions to get started by having fewer options to think about
- Better salespeople in less time

If an owner is concerned with missing out on potential revenue from prospects who demand a certain way of paying, they may create more membership options out of the belief that more options make it easier to increase revenue. On the level of the individual prospect, it is true that it's easier to capture one person's money when you have a pricing plan that's perfect for the person in front of you. However, the broad strokes would tell a different story.

Three people buying four-packs of classes might result in a total revenue of $240. What would it look like if no class packs were offered, and only unlimited membership options were presented? Well, if only one of those people bought an unlimited membership instead of a class pack and the other two bought nothing, an unlimited membership at $120 per month sold to a member who only stayed eight months and referred no one would produce $960 of revenue. That's four times the revenue from one third of the transactions, with no need to chase the members to get them back in and buy more class packs. Those numbers don't even reflect all the facts:

- Class-pack holders might repurchase in the future, but that is offset by the fact that many will not. Even many of those who do will wait a few weeks or months after their class pack runs out to purchase another.
- Some will allow their class packs to expire but still want to use them. Then when they eventually come in to work out, they will be upset when they can't use the expired passes.
- Class-pack holders are often less committed and less likely to bring in referrals who purchase actual memberships. If the non-recurring class-pack holders do bring in referrals, those referrals are also likely to want non-recurring class packs.
- Regular members encourage retention. Infrequent-use class-pack holders encourage going from facility to facility. The more transient, occasional users you have, the harder it is to have great retention. Higher retention always contributes to higher profit margins because it reduces the effort needed for marketing, follow up, sales, and new-member onboarding.

It also increases the ROI from marketing dollars invested, making us more likely to invest in marketing and better able to compete for growth.

Fewer options, more decisions

Have you ever noticed the difference between getting a McDonald's ice cream cone and one from the old-fashioned ice cream store?

There's a place called the Baked Bear in the neighborhood of Pacific Beach, San Diego. It's located just off the boardwalk. Behind one half of their glass cases, there are fourteen different flavors of ice cream. You'll see things like moose tracks, red velvet cake, cotton candy, and pistachio in a frosty array under the fluorescent lights. Behind the other half of the glass counter, piled in high stacks, there are about six different types of cookies. Flavors like white chocolate chip macadamia nut, chocolate chip brownie, and peanut butter cookie. My favorite is the half-baked doughnut. When you order the half-baked doughnut, they cut it in half and place it in a waffle iron to cook it the rest of the way. Finally, a scoop of ice cream goes inside the warm doughnut. It's incredible, especially after leg day.

There's usually a line, especially in the summer. If you were to watch that line while happily dripping a moose tracks doughnut hither and yon, you might notice a few things. For instance, even though the majority of the people arriving at the counter have been waiting at least ten minutes to place an order, they still don't know what they want. Have you had the white chocolate chip cookie before? What about the regular cookie with white chocolate chips? Each person in line likely spent five to twenty minutes on the walk or drive to the ice cream shop before the ten-minute wait in line surrounded by six to ten other Baked Bear regulars, all within arm's reach. This all occurs before the $4.50 decision over a menu of options that never changes. That's something like twenty minutes of time spent on a $4 decision with six minutes of oral pleasure hanging in the balance. That's more time to think about it than it takes to eat it, but when the person behind the counter asks what they want, they *still* need to think about it. Nuts!

Compare that to ordering the cone at McDonald's. When the guy behind the counter says, "Whaddya like?" I step up to the counter and say, "Vanilla ice cream." Sometimes, I'll say, "Chocolate." Other times, if I'm really feeling particularly squirrely, I'll say, "chocolate-vanilla swirl." However, you don't often observe the same phenomenon of a twenty-minute preparation period followed by indecision that exists at the Baked Bear.

The principle here is that the more options you have, the harder it is to choose, and the more likely someone is to say, "I need to think about it." That happens even over seemingly insignificant decisions. The more significant the potential impact of the choice, the more weight is pulling the logic and emotions of the prospect in multiple directions all at once. This leads to confusion and opens the door for indecision. Just like at the ice cream shop, the confused mind does not move forward.

Instead of creating membership options that serve the individual, create price packaging for the purpose of changing lives. Instead of selling people what they want out of fear, help them commit to what they need out of strength. Design your packaging and membership presentation for the success of your perfect clients, not for making everyone happy. Create simple options that employees can sell easily.

The rule of thumb here is that fewer options is always better. The same applies to lots of things in life.

I also suggest you make an electronic membership presentation. I prefer a simple slideshow that minimizes distraction. The ones I help clients build include a simple opening page with the company logo and maybe the tagline. A second page lists membership benefits in a particular format. A third page shows the simplest price options with key membership terms, which are always presented as benefits to the success of the new member, not as restrictions. The fourth and final page is a warm, fuzzy picture demonstrating the vibe of your community. You'll switch to this page to handle objections, if needed. This system is designed to make it easy for anyone to present memberships well. It will also make sure that each person presents membership options the same way each time.

Using an electronic presentation, if possible, makes sales easier when you can present options, sign an agreement, and collect a credit or debit card all in one spot. It's a small upgrade but conveys more permanence and value when presenting price than a piece of paper can, and typically encourages a seated position. Being seated makes it much easier to have a conversation with a potential new member. If your team is presenting memberships standing up, just the shift to discussing the membership investment on an electronic device while seated can produce a 10 percent increase in closing ratios. Ideally, you'll want to present the price using the same device you use to start a membership. That will create the smoothest transition from presentation to new member.

Presenting price with a presentation as opposed to just presenting verbally (without having any visual representation of the membership options) means that the salesperson will spend less energy thinking about what's next; this leaves more energy available to invest in listening to the person in front of them. When your system is consistent and simple, the level of reliance on the people who run the system is reduced.

What we are aiming for is consistency and simplicity. Managing people is complex enough, even with simple systems. Don't make it harder on yourself by trying to manage complex team members, complex prospects and complex systems. Create simple systems that reduce complexity and make it easier to manage people.

CHAPTER EIGHT

Four Segment Sales System - Embracing Objections

"It is not a daily increase, but a daily decrease.
Hack away at the inessentials."
– Bruce Lee

So we've arrived. After performing a needs assessment with deep listening skills and a proper price presentation, the stage is set! If the needs assessment and price presentation went really well, your new member will be ready to make a choice.

Objections occur less frequently when your needs assessment is very good, but they will still happen as part of the normal human decision-making process. The primary focus should remain on doing a great needs assessment, helping a prospect find clarity, and working through any hesitations while there, so objections don't arise after presenting the investment in membership. But even if that's done perfectly, objections will still occur. That's okay; it just means your prospect is not ready to give you a clear yes or no. It can also mean that their old habits are still fighting to keep them stuck. Either way, allowing a "maybe" instead of a yes or no is not serving them or you. The focus of the entire sales process has been to bring a person to a clear decision. Hearing a no is fine. Hearing a yes is great. Anything other than a clear yes or no means there's still work to do.

Objections can be very useful when used properly. For instance, when your team encounters objections, use them in the sales training environment. You can help the team to condition their mindset by discussing objections they encounter as a group. Ask your team, "What are some questions that could have drawn this objection out to address it during the needs assessment, before presenting the investment in membership?" They'll come up with a few, and then you can practice using those questions with other reps acting as prospects with similar objections. If you focus on learning from past failures, the frequency of encountering objections that the team doesn't automatically know what to do with will go down, and your close ratio will go up.

Objection Handling After Presenting Price

Do not fear or push back against hesitations or objections if they do come up after presenting the price of membership. They will come up from time to time, and they are a normal part of the progression for some prospects, especially prospects who have been stuck for some time. They are the ones who will need the most help overcoming objections. When objections do arise, what your team learned in the needs assessment gives them everything they need to help a prospect come to a clear choice. We'll use that information to help prospects overcome their own hangups and make a choice. Continually conditioning your team to address objections before price is presented is the most effective path. Singular focus on addressing objections early is the one thing that will make everything else in the sales process easier or unnecessary.

Let's contrast this with the dated, high-pressure sales pattern that people used to teach:

- Build rapport while trial closing
- Present price early, forcing objections to the surface
- Invest the majority of the time hammering away objections and pushing the prospect into a choice before the thin rapport reserves run out
- Close the deal and push for referrals using up any last bits of rapport
- Call it a success when an annual contract is signed

Here's how it looks when we meet a prospect wherever they are on the buyer's journey and draw them along the path so that a sale is just the natural result of their internal change:

- Invest the majority of the time in:
  - o Learning about their current situation
  - o Understanding the value to the prospect of changing their situation by asking about what they want to achieve and why those things matter to them
  - o Drawing out their reasons for why it isn't in their best interest to delay the decision or keep doing what they're currently doing
  - o Obtaining their partner's likely perspective
- Allowing the prospect to draw membership options out of us instead of us pushing it on the prospect
- Giving the prospect an easy way to bring friends in
- Calling it a success when the new member has been using the facility frequently for their first ninety days

If you're following that second outline well, you'll encounter objections much less often. But when you do encounter an objection, start by isolating it. Understand that most objections are the brain's tools for helping someone remain the same. To the survival instincts in the human mind, the "samer" it is, the "safer" it is. So, if you don't help a prospect contain and isolate the specific source of their reservation, their mind will continue to adapt ways of keeping them stuck. That's what's happening when we're trying to help someone make a choice, and it feels like nailing Jell-O to the wall.

A simple objection-handling sequence goes like this:

1. Mirror their objection statement to make sure there's total clarity: "So you want to ___?"
2. Make it okay (what I term "embracing an objection"): "Okay, take all the time you need to ___."
3. Isolate the objection: "Besides wanting to ___, is there anything else that would keep you from getting started?"
4. Obtain permission once all reasons for not coming to a choice are drawn out and isolated: "All right, is it okay with you if we work on a solution for that together?"
5. "If it were possible/would you," statement: "Okay, and if it were possible for us to find a solution for that and you're really happy with the solution, would you be willing to get started today?"
6. After they say, "Yes," loop back to what they said earlier in the needs assessment and insert a solution: "Okay. Earlier you said _____ is really important to you. Is that still true? Great, so, do you think if I could _____ [insert solution that addresses their needs] that would take care of everything for you? [Wait for their affirmation.] Great, I'm happy to do that for you. Let's go ahead and get you started!"

Isolating the objection in the first step reduces the likelihood of other objections popping up later and ensures that we've drawn out all of their hesitations. This sequence is what's called "building a bridge of 'yes.'" Notice, we are drawing several affirmative responses out of the prospect before working on their objection together. We've gotten an easy, "yes," in point one. We reply in a way that makes their desire to think about it okay in point two. This will be a positive thing in the mind of the prospect, and helps to continue to build the expectation that you will not judge them. If the entire needs assessment felt that way to the prospect, they will continue to be open with you here, rather than throwing out a fake reason to avoid making a choice. When we ask for their small commitment in point three, they will answer it easily.

Point four, in the sequence above, is the question that has the highest friction. Do not leave point four without hearing a confident "yes." If you don't get a confident, affirmative response, default to curiosity and ask about it. Make sure all reasons for hesitating are out in the open. Everything from there on is like coasting downhill. As the prospect moves in the correct direction, the friction is reduced, making point five much easier for them to say "yes" to. Only at this point is the tension fully resolved and the friction evaporated.

As you can see, the work you do in the needs assessment portion is crucial. If we don't do that well, we'll never know the prospect's potential reasons for overcoming their hesitation. In training environments, objections should be treated like a sign that the needs assessment could have been better. In this way, we are aiming for the best-case scenario while becoming prepared for more challenging scenarios.

After the objection is taken care of, select the membership option they said they'd lean toward when you asked earlier, "Hypothetically, which membership option would you lean toward if you were to get started?" Do *not* ask again which membership they'd like, because this will trigger parts of the mind we are not engaging with at the moment. They already said the type of membership that makes the most sense for them earlier, and there's no need to complicate it now. Now move to the first step in signing someone up, which should *not* be asking for a credit card. That can produce someone saying that they don't have their wallet with them. Instead of asking for a credit card right away, try this script:

1. Great, here's the heart rate monitor that comes with your membership.
2. Who should I set up as your emergency contact?
3. Okay, and is this the best phone number to keep on file?
4. Great, we'll be sending your membership agreement to this email address. Is that good, or would you prefer a different one?
5. All right, this first signature is for ___. [Get all the electronic signatures and initials needed on the membership agreement.]
6. Okay. I can put the investment on any type of credit card or debit card you'd like. [Let the new member know what the total charge will be and get a signature authorizing the charge before charging their card and moving on to the post sale process.]

The sequence used for addressing objections before moving on to signing the member up does a few things. First, in isolating the objection, it reduces the likelihood of other things popping up. Second, it ensures that we've drawn out all of their hesitations to making a choice. Third, this sequence is, again, "building a bridge of 'yes.'"

As you can see, the work you do in the needs assessment portion is crucial. If we don't do that well, we'd never know the prospects own reasons for overcoming their hesitation. In seeking to address this common objection before presenting price, we found out how long this prospect had been thinking about taking action. In training environments, objections should be treated like a sign that the needs assessment could have been better. In this way, we are aiming for the best case scenario while becoming prepared for more challenging scenarios. Be sure to access the online resources for this segment to get the objection-handling training sheet that you can print out and use to practice with. It's like having an answers guide that covers everything that will be on the "test." This way, when objections are encountered, the answers will be ready in advance. If you'd like the objection-handling training sheet, access the online resources now found at www.membershipsalesbook.com/resources.

CHAPTER NINE

Four Segment Sales System - Onboarding and Retention

"Make new friends, but keep the old.
One is silver, the other gold"
– Joseph Parry

Better lead generation connects us with leads earlier on in the buyer's journey. That requires better follow up and gets many people through the door who would not have come in on their own and who we never would have had the opportunity to connect with otherwise. The internal work we help a prospect progress through in fifteen minutes might have taken months or years to develop without that conversation. Improved lead generation creates a domino effect: it demands improvements in follow up, appointment setting, and sales processes. All of that means that we're going to also need improvements in our post-sale processes.

With weak marketing, weak lead nurturing, and weak sales, the new members we would be acquiring don't take as much effort to retain. If they were plants, they would be three-year-old saplings: you'd be able to plop those little guys in the ground, maybe give them a bit of water here and there, and they're good to go. With strong marketing, lead nurturing, and sales, we're changing lives that would otherwise be inaccessible. Now we're not only working with three-year-old, easy-to-grow saplings (the prospects who show up on their own) but with brand-new seedlings, too. These seedlings will not survive a heavy downpour, too much sun, or a few frosty mornings on their own, but with care, they will develop the resilience, habits, and willpower they did not have before. Their personal development, combined with visible results and the fortifications that come with integrating into a healthy community, will likely be enough to keep this sort of new member going.

Day one of a new membership is the most crucial retention opportunity and must be managed with intent. If you don't handle the first few weeks of each membership well, no other efforts will matter. It's way too late to think about retention on day one hundred when a new member is trying to cancel. Day one of all new memberships is the most important day for member retention.

This is why early-stage membership usage is one of the key stats in a fitness business. The more times a member visits in their first ninety days, the more likely they are to stay for the long term. Notice that on day one, when you just sold the membership, excitement on the part of the new member is at a peak. Also, pain levels are typically lower on day one than they're likely to be on day two and three. Most importantly, day one is the only day you can actually count on that new member being there. When that's done well, driving great average member retention through shifting seasons has a fighting chance.

This is why I always tell new trainers and coaches that it's not their job to push a new member as hard as they can on day one. Their job is making sure the new member is back on day two and three. Most new members need to hear this too. Everyone is tempted to "make up for lost time," but getting the most out of a membership is not about a few hard workouts. Help them optimize for a long-term shift of lifestyle by encouraging and ensuring that they take it easy in their first few workouts.

"Don't be afraid to throw up in the gym!" is good advice for us, but that advice is not for our new members.

Here's the plan for day one that will help your new members stick with good habits right away:

1. Schedule
2. Infiltrate
3. Acquire referrals

Many of your leads that join from marketing will not already be successfully engaged in a fitness lifestyle. This means that their habits and thoughts will not be supporting success in this area.

Your team will need to guide new members through some basic changes of schedule to help them focus on long-term goals while celebrating smaller wins along the way. This will help a new member become successful at making a lasting change. Unfortunately, people will sell or purchase a membership and think they have arrived, but we all know what happens if someone buys a membership and then does nothing. They are a cancellation waiting to happen, and are definitely not referring any new members. So, what has to happen for someone to take the next step of *using* a membership after buying it? The new member has to *plan* to use it. It sounds simple, but if someone is not currently successfully enjoying a fitness lifestyle, their planning skills likely need some help.

> *"By failing to prepare, you are preparing to fail."*
> *– Benjamin Franklin*

Schedule

Scheduling visits is what has to happen for someone to become consistent. We ourselves know what has to happen, but often those who join your facility have failed to develop good habits. In order to promote new habits, do your best to see a new member four times per week for the first two weeks.

Why four visits per week and not the traditional three? Because we're enforcing a habit every day. If you go to the gym three times per week, four times per week you're reinforcing the habit of *not* going to the gym. If someone regularly goes to the gym three times per week, they'll always have the friction of the habits formed on the other four days to fight against. There are always exceptions, but the people you see who are dedicated to a fitness journey typically have a habit of being active four or more times per week. So, at four visits per week, the scales have tipped in favor of retention.

I also like to help a new member block out one additional, optional workout time beyond the four crucial ones. If the new member needs to decide to substitute a day, it will already be available in their schedule. Note: this isn't a backup plan for when plan "A" fails and they miss a workout. It's an optional available time in their schedule for when they might choose, in advance, to substitute a day.

The early phases of a fitness journey carry a lot of opportunity, because the new member is already re-establishing habits. Later on, it's harder to change habits, kind of like how it's easier to keep a seedling growing straight at the beginning than it is to straighten the trunk of a full-grown tree.

To get the most out of this chance, have your team lead new members toward visiting *frequently* right away, but slowly work up to higher *intensity*. Your coach's efforts will need to go toward making sure the new member shows up tomorrow, not giving them a difficult workout today. They'll do this by focusing on keeping the new member's intensity low, making sure they are injury-free and building the habit of frequent use.

On day one, the moment someone joins, schedule the first two weeks' worth of workouts. Shoot for four days a week. Let your team know that not every new member will be able to do this, but encourage them to influence a new member toward this goal as often as possible.

Four hours of actual workout time and thirty minutes of commute is very possible, especially when you consider that those six hours represent less than four percent of their week. For anyone willing to prioritize their health and fitness, four times a week isn't much to ask. Six hours invested in the gym improves happiness and sleep, reduces stress, and makes most people more productive. That increased productivity means investing six hours per week in health and fitness doesn't reduce one's ability to accomplish what one set out to do each week—it usually increases it. If your team feels that four visits per week isn't too much to ask, they'll convey that in the way they ask it.

Planning the first two weeks on a written document is best, because it is something the member is meant to take with them. Once you've filled in the schedule, encourage the new member to put that schedule somewhere they will see it multiple times each day—not just in their phone, but on their fridge or taped next to where they put their keys. This bit of commitment will make them much more likely to follow through with the plan. The schedule sheet can also be used to list their goals and core drivers, so frequent attendance and their motivations are repeatedly associated.

Beyond the frequency of visits, we should aim for as regular a pattern as possible. Visiting at random times does not allow for your body's natural rhythm to acclimate, and it only makes it harder to form habits. What we want is for our body's natural cycles to create the expectation of exercise at a certain time of day. This way, our members will be working with the natural orientation of chemical processes their bodies are already trying to create patterns around. People who have been in the fitness industry for a while will note that the early morning crew is most consistent. They are the members you can count on, partly because at that time of day, there are fewer things that can get in the way and disturb the pattern. It's also because their thoughts have not been pulled in hundreds of directions yet, so their focus is clearer. Choosing to prioritize things that are valuable but not urgent gets harder as the day wears on.

Use these concepts as a baseline and optimize a post sale ritual that works well for you. It should happen each time a new member joins.

Infiltrate

"Infiltrate," in this context, refers to injecting your systems into someone else's life, much like a virus. We want to start appearing in as many areas of a new member's life as possible. Once you've cleared their mind of all objections, limiting beliefs, and poor priorities, they break new ground internally—which results in the purchase of a membership externally. Invite your team to keep in mind that new members come to us for help with making progress in their life, not with help in buying a membership. Since we're there to help members get what they came for, we'll need to help members plant the seeds of new habits, or things will slowly return to chaos.

Infiltrating someone's life in as many areas as possible produces natural reminders you can use to influence their habit formation. We want to encourage a member toward greater identification with who they are becoming instead of getting stuck with who they have been. We can help in these areas by creating as many subtle reminders as possible that pop up in their lives outside the gym. New member packets are a great place to start. I like to include things like:

- A printed paper schedule
- Car window transparencies
- A list of local companies that provide discounts to members
- A printed list of key contacts
- A new member "buddy pass" gift card (explained in detail in the next segment)
- Branded water bottle

Before the new members leave, I like to help them get into a Facebook group for posting questions, getting feedback, staying connected with the community, hearing about upcoming events, etc. Then be sure to help them download the app if your facility has one. I'm a big fan of giving them a keychain barcode for checking in, too. I'll often recommend using less inexpensive things, like branded t-shirts, and other gear as standard "join day one incentives" for new people who visit. This is better than offering discounts to get someone to join because they accomplish similar goals and promote retention way better than offering a membership discount to people who join.

Get creative with these things and pick what your team will have fun giving out and your members will have fun getting. If the new member packets are fun to give and fun to get, you won't have to put out much effort in monitoring that system. Make sure they're already put together and ready to go. Do not get caught unprepared for a new membership—expect new people to join all the time. These new member packets should be easy to hand off as the last thing a new member gets on the way out of the door their first day. Some more advanced retention tools include things like specialized equipment, heart rate monitors, and other tech tools. Evaluate the cost of things like that as an investment. Tools like that won't always make sense for every facility.

The way something starts and the way it ends will be the most significant impression of your facility for most people, so consider this phase a key moment for making an intentional investment of energy. Even if these processes improve average retention by just a month or two, it is reasonable to expect a positive return on investment from them.

Acquire referrals

An effective post-sale system will focus on promoting immediate referrals and frequent use of the facility from day one. Of the two, early and frequent use of the facility is the priority, so people will be more likely to get what they came for and therefore drive the average member lifetime value up. When average member lifetime value is high, acquisition costs will remain low in comparison. More profit and more people helped is the result.

On the subject of costs, I find that keeping costs *reasonably* low is much easier and more fun than working to keep costs *very* low. Focusing the majority of the effort on retention instead of on saving money is following a higher calling. It's more sustainable, more enjoyable, and more effective, because relying on low cost to get good margins only benefits the owner. Focusing on high retention benefits the owner, the members, and your team, so it's much easier to motivate a team toward this objective.

Giving a member the ability to bring a friend right away in the first few days is a crucial element in retention and in creating a culture that encourages referrals. Getting a referral right away helps a new member develop habits of using the facility. It's easier to be successful with the support of a friend, which is why referrals do not only produce more members—they also help with retention. This is one element, like sales skills, that impacts multiple key areas of a fitness business.

Rather than asking for a referral, give the gift of *free access for a friend* when a new member joins. Rather than trying to drag a cold prospect in, use your new member as the communication channel. The gift of free access for a friend needs to be tangible, hard to forget, and convey value. Optimally, use a format similar to a gift card. This way, you'll be able to physically hand it to a new member. Rather than floating in the background of someone's life, it is now an object (with an expiration date within two weeks of the date of issue).

Make sure the pass conveys value. Print it on nice paper. It should include a week or more of free access for the guest. You'll also want to write in the name of the person who will get the free access, because this forces thought and communication about the gift to occur between the prospect and the team member. That will make it more memorable for the new member because they've picked the person it's for.

Whatever you do, don't underestimate the value of referrals. Consider these two hypothetical scenarios: Some people join a gym, pay $100 per month, and stay for twelve months, resulting in $1,200 of revenue. Other members pay $100 per month, stay for twenty-four months (or more), and refer three friends, resulting in $2,400 of revenue from just the first member, not including the revenue from the referred members. If each of the three referred members were to stay for twelve months each, that's an additional $3,600 of revenue that all stemmed from one new member.

Likely, the friends the member referred who stayed twenty-four months contributed to the retention of the original member. Because referrals and retention are synergistic, they can make the difference between $1,200 of revenue from one new member and $6,000 in total from four new members.

Do not plan on instant, astronomical results from these strategies. Most of the impacts will come long after you'd remember to associate the effort with your results. Use what I've shared to get something better than the post-sale process you have currently. All your team members will be trained to adopt it. Over time, it will get better and better. All the members from that point on will be retained a bit longer. Your goal is to generate a notch or two more revenue than you did in the past. Eventually, the scales will tip when more people were brought on from the new way in your facility than people who were not. By then, the referred members will be referring members. They will add to the referrals from new members who came in from other sources. Those referrals will be more likely to become part of your core tribe.

The core tribe consists of the people who have been there forever and who will be there forever. They are the ones who know everyone, come often, and add to the atmosphere of your facility. More upfront referrals increase the likelihood of your new members becoming part of the core tribe, because referred members are more social and are likely to be high retention themselves. On top of that, referred members increase the retention of the members who refer them.

As the core tribe grows, the culture of your facility will orient toward members staying longer and referring more often. That's just how things will be, because that's what the average member does. The expectation is that people who join will refer and will stick around forever. When that's the expectation of members and staff, that's how everyone treats everyone and more retention is the result. The core tribe naturally draws your new members into the social circles of the facility. That will take on a momentum of its own over time, but you'll have to get the ball rolling by retraining staff and inviting referrals.

Retaining members is much more profitable than acquiring new ones. Referred members do not have the same acquisition costs as members you had to spend marketing dollars to acquire. The long-term result of focusing on retaining and referrals is worth it. Facilities that do this well find that the revenue of the average member is very high, and the cost compared to the amount of membership revenue drops because acquisition costs stay low.

For instance, if the average member is paying $135 per month, stays for fourteen months, and buys $75 of additional services, their value is $1,965. Now let's imagine you have a 20 percent referral rate. This means that one in every five members successfully refers a friend. One fifth of $1,965 is $393. When we add average referral revenue to average member value, we get a total average $2,358 of revenue per member. Compare that to another facility with the same monthly rate, the same amount of average additional services sold, but with an average retention of eight months instead of fourteen and an average referral rate of 10 percent instead of 20 percent. The total value of their average member paying the exact same rate is only $1,270.50, about half of the value of the average member in the first example. The difference in profit margin will be even more significant than that. This is because the gym with the average retention of eight months and fewer referrals will have to spend a lot more energy on marketing and sales commission to keep their bucket full.

By emphasizing retention and referrals, you will have better margins than your competition does. This makes it easier to acquire members at a profit and easier to spend energy on developing your systems. That cycle will gain momentum and help you become the most profitable facility in your area. The systems for growth and retention will become part of the culture of your business. It won't be an accident, either—it will be built on systems that were constructed with intent. Things that don't happen by accident are replicable. When you have a model that's worth copying, you'll be giving me a call to help you build a pre-sale system so your franchisees get members before they open their doors!

CHAPTER TEN

Training Your Team

"Quality is not an act, it is a habit."
– Aristotle

Finding growth and development to be motivating is one of the key things I look for when hiring team members of all sorts, especially for sales roles. Recognizing the value of development and being motivated to grow are characteristics of the elite. The ones who want to grow will be more satisfied with their role, and their performance will increase as a result. The ones who aren't interested in growth simply won't fit in with the culture you create.

Motivation basics

A good sales training process will contain a little bit of instruction on the framework of the needs assessment, price presentation, objection handling, and post-sale processes. A little bit of instruction with a lot of practice is the winning combination. The goal of your instruction in each of those four segments is to outline a pathway for them to happen in the same, repetitive pattern, regardless of who's making the sale.

However, you can't force a team to do that. Leadership in sales doesn't look like a demand placed on others. It looks more like an invitation to help the individuals on your team step into a more powerful version of themselves. There should be some tension to progress, but not because the people above the sales team are pushing them. The tension to progress should always come from positive motivators, not negative ones. Basically, your team will need a clear reason for wanting to improve in these areas, or you shouldn't expect them to improve at all. Establish a culture of ownership that champions failure as part of the developmental process. Then, structure compensation so that each person making sales does not view themselves as a traditional employee. Instead, they should feel more like the master of their own mini-business within your business. Their role should have slightly more open boundaries than a traditional employee, such as the ability to innovate and create sales opportunities. Help them develop as an internal entrepreneur—or an "intrapreneur"—whose personal goals align with the success of your business.

Keep compensation as simple as possible and align it with your goals. As an owner, you want to acquire and retain members, so align your salespeople's mini-businesses with your goals. Create an immediate reward for acquisition, but make the focus long-term retention. In doing this, you'll establish the alignment of your goals and their goals. Also, do not create competitions that pit members of your team against each other. If you do decide to offer a reward for achieving a larger goal (like hitting a monthly or quarterly goal), make it a team goal, not an individual one.

Assessing your team

With the most basic guidelines for motivating your team in place, let's move on to evaluating the individuals on your team. Here's a short list of questions to help you evaluate each team member within the area of sales. This test will help you identify the target of what to aim for when helping your salespeople develop. It should be applied to anyone who is responsible for starting memberships. Quickly evaluate each of them in the following five areas:

Needs Assessment:

Ineffective: a team member who does most of the talking in sales conversations with prospects.

Effective: a team member whose prospects do most of the talking because they habitually ask about a prospect's current situation, why that matters to them, their goals, and the implications of achieving those goals *before* presenting price.

Membership Benefits:

Ineffective: a team member who talks about how great the product is in hopes the prospect will think it's great too.

Effective: a team member who shares relevant benefits that apply to the prospect's specific situation so their prospects consistently feel the product offered is the right vehicle for achieving their desires.

Price Presenting:

Ineffective: a team member who lacks confidence, presents four or more membership options, or doesn't consistently express the key terms of membership agreements as benefits.

Effective: a team member who consistently presents investment options without hesitation in a way that conveys confidence to the prospect. They do so in a simple format, along with the key terms of your membership agreements being presented as benefits.

Objection Handling:

Ineffective: a team member who struggles to overcome common objections, appears nervous when handling objections, or doesn't even try.

Effective: a team member who hears objections infrequently because they've learned to anticipate and eliminate the most common objections like, "I want to think about it," "It costs too much," or "I want to talk with my partner about it" before presenting price. However, if objections do come up, they address them in a relaxed manner with questions and reminders of what the prospect has already said.

Retention and Referrals:

Ineffective: a team member whose new members join and leave that first day without referring and without a plan for success.

Effective: a team member whose new members nearly always walk out with an ideal weekly schedule, plans to return on a specific day and time, and often refer new members.

If you've evaluated each team member this way, it will help you identify areas of potential growth. Focus your effort on mentoring one team member (the one you recognize is the most eager to learn and the most enjoyable to interact with) into greatness—meaning, they would be scored as "effective" in five out of the five areas outlined above. The moment that person becomes effective in one of the five categories, they should immediately start teaching that skill to other team members by practicing with them. Rapid individual and group development leading to a cultural shift is what we're after, here. This happens faster when every person has someone to learn from, someone who is in stride with them, and someone they are teaching.

No gray space

Without clearly defining the standards of what's effective in an area like membership sales, you're inviting the entire team to slump to the lowest common denominator. If your salespeople would be evaluated as ineffective in several of the areas mentioned, there are two options: do the work of training them to become closers, or fire them right now. There is no middle ground.

We can't allow middle ground because if we provide ourselves the comfort of allowing team members to be ineffective at sales, we are creating a continuous stream of feedback communicating that being ineffective at sales is acceptable. This will not help your team develop. The good news is that deciding whether to fire or train an individual or team is simple: just ask yourself if it has been your priority to help your team become effective at sales or not. Helping your team develop in this area looks like putting significant, regular effort into group and individual sales practice. If it's a priority, group sales practice will happen weekly at minimum and individual sales training daily. For new sales reps, individual sales training should be happening after each of their first thirty sales conversations at a minimum. If you have not done that, don't start with firing team members who aren't effective, start with firing the old version of yourself who didn't prioritize sales training and hire the new version of yourself who does. Give yourself no middle ground. It's one or the other. Have you prioritized sales training or have you not? In any case, do not allow yourself wiggle room. If you do not hold yourself to a clear standard, you'll never be able to require clear standards of your team. The future lives you're called to impact, and the impact they have on those around them, is at stake. There is no gray space when someone visits your gym. Either the life that needed your help is changed forever, or it isn't.

Three Key Questions

The next stop in maintaining a healthy environment for the development of sales skills is developing the habit of asking these three key questions after a sales opportunity:

1. What did I do well?
2. What could I have done differently?
3. What will I do better next time?

This ritual may seem trite, but are you actually taking the time to use it? The truth is that anyone can get better at anything with practice *and* evaluation, but practice alone won't do the trick. Practice without evaluation is dangerous, because we can practice doing something the wrong way and become worse. This habit of assessing our teams and ourselves will prevent that.

Years of daily persistence in this practice has made a massive difference in my life. Most people spend their days darting from one shallow task to the next. This incessant buzz leaves little opportunity for reflection. They're all growing, but who knows in what direction. This lifestyle is normal now. It's why people find meditation to be so revolutionary. There's something wild about sitting still and being quiet in a world where we don't ever do it.

The point is this: train your team to take a few moments after each sales opportunity to assess their successes and failures. The key is to start and end with what you did well and visualize what you'll do differently next time. That way, their brains will focus on what was done well. This will help them build the habits just by visualizing them. During this visualization, encourage your team to experience feelings. Always end this visualization with imagining the prospect joining and experiencing incredible, life-changing results that reverberate out into the lives around them.

There's this funny thing about the mind. Our brains and bodies don't know the difference between imagination and reality. That means that within the controlled environment of the imagination, we can alter our habits. Our lives are a result of our habits. We're basically asleep at the wheel for the majority of the day. Most of our energy is expended at the direction of unconscious habits and patterns. Thoughts and emotions produce actions that our brains are incessantly seeking to program into habits. Let's put our team's thoughts to good use. By building improvements into our thought habits, they will result in automatic actions. Through this process, we're training our teams to continually hone skills and condition the intentions, beliefs, and habits of success rather than letting them get stuck on the failures.

The simplest way to train this habit is to ask the three key questions after each sales opportunity. Do this one-on-one with team members until they're doing it on their own. You want this to become part of the culture of your community. You'll know that this has happened when your team members begin voluntarily doing this on their own both in your business and in their own daily lives. When that cultural shift happens, it will keep going without you. Then you're free to take a vacation or open a second facility because even while you're gone, the culture you've built will produce growth. It's going to take discipline to engrain this habit, but discipline, oddly enough, is what lines the path to more freedom. If you're not willing to ask your team these questions habitually, don't expect them to ask themselves these questions. By the way, if this practice is the only thing you use from this book, your time here will have been well spent.

The goal of evaluation is to produce this perpetual cycle:

1. Identify opportunities for improvement
2. Take action on the most vital opportunities for improvement
3. Identify and champion progress as early and as often as possible

The third point is the most important. Our mentality in evaluating is not to focus on deficiencies. That is only a slight deviation from the cycle mentioned above, but it has the potential to change everything. Instead of focusing on finding weaknesses, instead, it is our job to focus on finding and championing strength and progress, particularly new strength and progress. I invite you to absorb this mentality and spend your life's energy habitually championing areas where your team members and everyone around you are found to be growing or powerful. You can begin extending this type of growth motivation to others by practicing on yourself with the following questions:

1. Where have I grown in the last week?
2. What do I know now that I didn't a year ago (or more)?
3. What strengths have I developed that I wouldn't have expected ten years ago?

CHAPTER ELEVEN

Elite Communication

"Most people do not listen with the intent to understand;
they listen with the intent to reply."
– Stephen R. Covey, The 7 Habits of Highly Effective
People: Powerful Lessons in Personal Change

Here, we're going to encounter the building blocks of elite communication that produce sales. This is meant to provide you with language for training your team and with concepts to steep the culture of your business in.

A prospect's progress along the buyer's journey toward a changed life can take months or years without the support of a great salesperson. Without help, many prospects will get lost along the way and never reach the destination. It's up to us to change that.

That is quite an undertaking... It's an even higher calling to become great at training a team to do this. But, once you get into it, you'll be surprised at how easy it is with the process I'll be sharing with you. Besides that, you're the number one most equipped person to do this in your business.

With razor-sharp marketing and lead nurturing, we will bring buyers in. The better our lead generation and nurturing is, the closer to the start of the journey the average buyers will be. That's a great thing, because it's our chance to change a lot of lives without requiring them to go through years of pain before the change occurs. With good practice, you and every single person on your team will become much better at taking the organic thought processes of years and condensing it down to minutes. I can say "every single person" with confidence, because our mind is just like a muscle. We can each become better at anything we choose to focus on, so there isn't a single person in the world who can't become better at sales.

Just to highlight this fact, I often ask owners if their business could become just a tiny bit better at sales by focusing on sales training. The answer, of course, is a resounding "Yes." Could an incremental improvement in sales training result in us helping just one more person this year? Of course it could! If each of us did that with just one extra person this year, we'd each be changing the course of *years* of other people's lives. How many years of life could be totally changed (or even *saved*) collectively in one year, or five, or ten? The answer is in the millions.

When we doggedly focus on just helping one more person, the skills to help thousands are the result. If we start by focusing on the thousands, we'll miss the opportunities of the present that would have led us to helping the thousands. There are some lives out there that only you and your business are made to connect with. You are in the process of being given those chances moment by moment. Some lives you encounter will only be changed forever if your tools are as ready as they can be. What could be more valuable than changing someone's life forever? That is the heart of a healthy sale and is the core of why sales training matters. With investment in this area, the old ceiling of your team's abilities will become the floor.

How to release the habit of listening to respond

Most people are in the habit of thinking about what they want to say next in a conversation while the person they are talking with is still speaking. Instead of listening to understand the other person, they are listening only to respond. Besides being obviously self-centered, this is one of the worst things you can do in a sales environment.

After listening to dozens of prospects, someone could easily predict a good portion of what is going to come up the moment a sales conversation with a new prospect begins. It becomes very easy to give in and let our brains wander. It's more interesting to us to think about what we're going to say. Listening to everything that's being said in the moment when it's mostly things we've heard before is not satisfying, but there's an easy way to ingrain healthy habits before your trainees feel the temptation to let their minds wander: choose to be curious.

Be curious about the person you are speaking with, no matter where you are or who you're talking to. *Choose* to be curious. Do this especially with people and conversations you find boring. You'll be surprised at the meaning you'll find in conversations that would have otherwise been boring. This will cause good listening to happen naturally.

Sometimes, even when we are listening, we get stuck in the habit of listening to respond. Doing this is so ingrained that many of us are not comfortable with pauses in conversation, so much so that most people feel anxious pressure to fill the silence. That feeling of pressure in silent pauses is a great indicator that there's an opportunity to improve listening skills. Instead of rushing to respond quickly, allow natural pauses between someone's statement or question and your reply. We cannot allow bad programming to dictate the cadence of our connection with people.

The useless "normal" of listening to respond quickly reduces our closing averages and ruins the ability to develop some key sales skills. So, diverge. Refuse to float passively in the current of society. Stop being normal. Start by actively choosing to be curious about the person in front of you instead of listening to respond. Allow pauses between sentences on purpose and become comfortable with a slower cadence of conversation. You will see that start to happen with you and your team by implementing some of the principles we'll explore here.

Silence is your friend

We're going to look at the curious talent of becoming comfortable with silence. Most people don't do this. That's what makes it a tool of the elite. Allowing silence in conversations is the simplest thing you can do to increase your sales. First, pauses in conversation are related to being a good listener. Good listeners do not listen to respond. They do not talk over the speaker's thoughts. Instead, they just wait so the speaker has to keep going. We actually have to become good at shutting up here and there to be good at listening. What a novel thought! It's obvious, but not practiced. Let's change that together.

Just like anything, the more we practice, the better we become. More silence equals better listening skills, without effort. In terms of seeking simple, sustainable solutions, this is one of my favorites.

It's obvious that pauses will help with listening, but there are several underlying benefits you'll want to point out. Have you ever noticed what comes right at the end of a sentence? Yes! There it is—not the punctuation. The simple blank space. This is always found in writing. Pauses between sentences provide space for clarity as someone moves from one expression of thought to the next. Without the space after the punctuation, the sentence would convey less meaning. Why not allow space in our speaking too? (Insert pause, for dramatic effect...)

The space at the end of a prospect's sentence and before the beginning of ours shouldn't be rushed. It is valuable because you'll be asking questions that cause prospects to think, often out loud. That's what happens in Elite Communication. We're seeking to help prospects draw out their own, new conclusions. That's how we act as a catalyst in the process that leads them to their own decision—a decision that, ideally, happens to align with our goals.

When learning this, I forced myself to count to three after each prospect ended a normal sentence before replying. I made myself count to five each time a prospect expressed a significant thought. A great way to practice this with your sales teams is in role play scenarios.

When I started practicing the art of silence, there was an immediate increase in what I call "gushing." This is when a prospect shares things from deep levels that they may not have ever shared before. Often, they have not even fully explored those thoughts themselves until that moment. It's what happens when the prospect feels listened to and interesting.

Let's teach our salespeople to allow for pauses in conversation. Tell your team that as they ask questions and prospects begin to think out loud, they won't be pushy. Instead, they will step into the role of the expert guide.

The bottom line is that confused minds do not move forward. As prospects work through the jungle of their minds, expressing and reiterating thoughts, they should have the space to do so until they are satisfied. What's happening under the surface is that their clarity is growing. As clarity develops, the ramifications of the options in front of them become clear. Clarity then produces confidence to move forward. A foggy thought doesn't leave anyone feeling strong and assured, but once a thought is clarified, moving forward is the natural result.

This is a great strategy for making sales and changing lives. We don't want to leave any lingering thoughts or "loose strings" in the prospect's mental landscape. We're looking to grow their sense of inner strength. That effort is nourished by clear, congruent thought processes. Success, in this regard, is externally indicated by a concise and satisfying expression of thoughts on the part of the prospect. Pause and wait until you notice that this has happened. It's like a rope. Pushing a rope isn't a great use of energy, just like pushing a prospect.

By the end of the conversation, the prospect's internal sense of confidence will have been built. We've given them protected space to think and express themselves. The clarity and confidence alone is a huge gift. Even if they don't join, you've still helped someone make progress. When a prospect can produce a precise description of where they are and where they'd like to be with confidence and conviction, that's the majority of the battle. From this sure psychological footing, it's much easier to draw out how the prospect's desired changes will impact their lives. The feelings that come with this expression is where the true drivers of change are found. These sacred gems are buried deep, in places your prospects must approach with confidence in order to approach at all.

In elite sales circles, the practice of silence is taught and developed, but what I've found is that almost no one focuses on it in fitness membership sales—I think because many of us focus instead on how great the workouts are. We're more comfortable talking about the ambiance of the studio or the quality of the equipment. It's much safer for us to focus on what we have.

When learning a new, others-centered form of connection, your ego will fight it. The fight will be hard enough to produce physical stress and anxiety. Your heart rate might elevate. Your skin might perspire. As a moment of silence becomes deafening, you might want to blurt out something. Notice what that something is. It will probably be something about why a potential new member should love what you built. "You'll love it here because of ___ [insert self-validating, ego-feeding trash here]." If you notice similar hurdles, press on. Keep going past the internal resistance. Your ego may throw fits at the lack of attention, but on the other side there's more freedom and more lives to be changed.

Indicators of Strength in the area of Communication

So, what are some indicators that you (and your sales team, by extension) have achieved Elite Conversation?

First, mutual respect for silence. For this to happen, silence must be granted existence by both the salesperson *and* the prospect. The salesperson will lead in allowing the space at the end of sentences to exist, and the prospect will follow suit and offer the same respect.

Second, Deep Listening. This kind of listening occurs best when we're focusing all of our perception on listening to fully absorb both what's being said and what's *not* being said. For instance, if you say to someone, "How are you doing?" That can sound like a statement or a question. If it sounds like a statement, you'll get a trite reply like, "I'm great, you?" It can also sound like a very compassionate, sincere question. In which case, the empathetic asker will tune in to the energy of the reply and likely draw more out of the person they're speaking with. Conversations are much more complex than most people notice. This skill is about intentionally getting better at tuning in to the symphony of fluctuating rapport, chemical interactions, and incessant, unconscious observations occurring below the surface of any conversation. We are improving our ability to change lives and close sales as a result. We will notice these things with less effort when, as we discussed earlier, we listen without any of our energy going into our future reply.

Let's encourage our teams to focus on intently tuning in to what others are communicating by hearing both what they're saying and what they're not saying. This particular skill is what I call "deep listening."

Deep listening is indicated by a sense of intense presence. People will describe it as being able to "feel" the conversation. This is in reference to a greater awareness of fluctuating rapport levels and the prospect's emotions. When we step into this state, there is a level of unconscious congruence between the people in the conversations. This congruence grows trust and elevates the salesperson's ability to hear what their prospects aren't saying. This is what people label intuition, but just like any muscle, it can be trained. As an elite salesperson, it *must* be trained, by habitually focusing on hearing and understanding everything a prospect is and isn't saying.

Third, an 80/20 balance of words. That means the prospect should do 80 percent or more of the talking, and we should do 20 percent or less. What's so interesting is that when we ask a question and just shut up, the prospect speaks while processing. Then, they express what they processed while speaking, as long as we stay silent. Eventually, they'll sum it all up in a concise, honest, and satisfying statement.

Our job is to make space for internal progression, clarity, and security. Buying a membership is a natural result of their new internal state.

Fourth, the rule of three to five. Instead of quickly moving the conversation from thing to thing like a teenager flicking through social media, condition yourself and your team to ask a minimum of three questions on each topic of conversation before moving on to the next topic. If we force ourselves to pay attention like we care, eventually, we will. Practice this in social settings, just for fun. You'll be amazed at how people open up to you.

With this skill, you'll always be able to have a great conversation with anyone, because everyone's favorite topic of conversation is themselves. Developing your ability to ask progressively deeper questions instantly produces high levels of rapport and trust. It also means that you'll spend the majority of your time listening and strengthening your intuition. It just so happens that when you exhibit interest in people and are good at asking questions, you are more likeable, a better conversationalist, and make more sales.

The following examples will give you a picture of the difference.

Listening to respond:

Doug: What do you do for your workouts?
Sherri: I like to walk around the neighborhood.
Doug: Okay, and what brought you in?
Sherri: Oh, I've just always noticed this place.
Doug: Got it. Well, what kinds of goals do you have?
Sherri: I'm just looking to tone up a bit.
Doug: What have you tried in the past?
Sherri: Zumba and a little spin.
Doug: What do you do for work?

While these are all good questions, it is boring conversation. It doesn't create a connection with a prospect. Besides that, Doug isn't learning any of the deeper undercurrents that are more important.

BORING! This surface-level small talk is absolutely worthless. It's a pointless waste of time and insulting to the person stuck in the conversation.

Here's an example of how a conversation would sound with the same prospect, but this time we're going deeper in each topic. Here are the kinds of things that would be likely to surface:

Doug: What do you do for your workouts?
Sherri: I like to walk around the neighborhood.
Doug: Oh, that's great, which neighborhood?
Sherri: The one that's on the other side of this plaza.
Doug: Wow, you're really close. How long of a walk do you think that might be?
Sherri: It's only about six or seven minutes. I walked here today.
Doug: Right on. So how are the walks going for you?
Sherri: They're okay.
Doug: They're okay?
Sherri: Yeah, I enjoy them, but I feel like I might need to step up the intensity a
notch or two.
Doug: Really, what makes you say that?
Sherri: Well, I've been looking to tone up a bit, and I haven't been making much progress.
Doug: Got it. So how long has it been like that?
Sherri: About three years.
Doug: Okay, and why not just stay where you are and keep walking?
Sherri: Well, my mother had osteoporosis. My doctor says I'm at a fairly high risk, and I need to start strength training.
Doug: Okay, so it sounds like you're looking to tone up a bit and increase bone density. Why are those things important to you?
Sherri: I've just watched my mother deteriorate over the years. She isn't able to play with my kids. I want to be able to keep up with my grandkids.

Notice, this is all from one topic of conversation: "What do you do for your workouts?" Doug simply asked follow-up questions relating to each statement Sherri made. He didn't didn't change the topic. The conversation flowed naturally. In the first example, there were five unique topics that would all have been covered in less than a minute:

- What do you do for your workouts?
- What brought you in?
- What kinds of goals do you have?
- What have you tried in the past?
- What do you do for work?

Imagine if someone were to ask three to five follow-up questions on each of those topics. They wouldn't have to go through so many topics to get the answers needed, the information shared would be layers deep instead of surface level, and the conversation would have flowed naturally because of the interest in the prospect as a person.

People slip into asking single questions and go from topic to topic because it feels safer. This is a habit many people have without realizing. We call it "light conversation" or "small talk," a cute little name in a weak attempt to mask reality. The truth is that people ask other people questions like this because they want to bounce from topic to topic in hopes of coming across a topic of common interest. That way, they can talk about something they both care about. That's how people talk when they don't really care about the other person, and are mostly looking to entertain themselves.

Surface-level talk is a great way to kill your closing ratio. It comes from a habit of self-centered thinking.

Ask yourself and your team these questions to help you spark discussion and exploration of this topic. You'll have a hard time answering these questions if you and your team are in dire need of developing their listening skills:

- Do you and your team experience pauses after sentences end? If you do, ask yourself and your team about what sorts of things they've experienced or noticed in these moments of silence in some of their recent sales conversations.
- Have you noticed people re-expressing themselves, essentially using you as a sounding board until they find their own clarity? Have you noticed how this builds a prospect's confidence in and appreciation for you? How are you intentionally encouraging this in your sales conversations?
- Are you observing that prospects are doing 80 percent or more of the talking with the salespeople in your facility?

Bringing Silence, Deep Listening and Asking Good Questions Together

Early in my sales training career, I recognized that the more often my team's silence, deep listening and good questions came together, the more memberships we sold. Later on, I found that this rule applies to all sales in general. When these elements converge, sales begin to happen (seemingly) on their own, with little apparent effort on our part. Once these habits are established, sales takes much less effort.

Make sure you're using the online resources from this segment for practical tools that will help you and your team put this information into practical action steps.

CHAPTER TWELVE

Identifying or Creating an Elite Membership Salesperson

"Nothing in the world can take the place of persistence. Talent will not; nothing is more common than unsuccessful men with talent. Genius will not; unrewarded genius is almost a proverb. Education will not; the world is full of educated derelicts. Persistence and determination alone are omnipotent. The slogan, 'Press On' has solved and always will solve the problems of the human race."
– Calvin Coolidge

Each of the three characteristics we're about to explore enable a person to become and remain successful in sales. Without a blend of these three traits, a team member won't consistently be successful in sales even with the best instruction.

We have all noted the ability of one person to impact the atmosphere around them. These people are good at shifting the mood and spreading their mentality to others. If we create a shift in mentality for others, the shift can leave as quickly as it came. You might notice that this can happen in whole teams or even entire organizations.

Our state of mind can change quickly in the short term, for the better or for the worse—but in the long term, how we have repeatedly chosen to be in each moment will become established as habits. Only then will someone's mood become a mentality and start producing fruit.

Success for salespeople is the fruit of their consistent mentality. Yes, they do have to work to maintain their mentality, but the key is that they are reliably successful in this endeavor, regardless of the situation. This regular success in mentality is possible because of the strength of their underlying habits. The key here is choosing to make consistent investments over time.

Not everyone is willing to make that choice, which is why people say you either have sales skills or you don't. But the mind is a muscle, and we can develop any traits we choose to. All it takes is consistent investment. To champion the truth that we have the ability to influence everything in our lives removes the ability to shift blame, rejects the easy path and rips the safety blanket off all shortcomings. The responsibility to produce a better tomorrow is on us. The responsibility to cultivate better salespeople who change lives is also on us.

Tenacity

The first characteristic is Tenacity, the ability to stick to something regardless of challenge, failure or setback. An indicator that this trait exists is a resilient strength that comes from taking bold risks over and over, with or without success. The tenacious are courageously determined when tested beyond the limits of boldness. They are some of the best salespeople.

Do not look for great sales to come from weak people who are subject to the environment around them. The tenacious become tenacious by not accepting the limits. Strength and growth are born from struggle. Without struggle, people will not grow. Being handed something reduces confidence. Earning something builds it. When you're hiring salespeople, look for the ones who think growing the individual makes the environment better, the ones who like to influence others and, through that influence, impact their environment.

Looking chaos in the eye without questioning one's own worth is what enables a person to learn while maintaining a Winner's Mentality. People who do not attach their value to external failure or success are free to choose and act at a rapid rate while remaining open to development, regardless of the outcomes. The best salespeople think this way and grow faster than their peers because of it.

Those seeking an excuse for mediocrity will mislabel success as a random gift. Success *is* a gift, but there is *nothing* random about it. Success in sales and business is the natural result of the person who takes more risks than their peers. To the outside observer, it will look like luck. Hire the "lucky" salespeople.

In practical terms, invest in people who love to learn, are eager to try new things, and aren't afraid of being wrong. It's a good sign if your potential new hire is able to love what they learn from failures and can move forward undaunted. This is why trained interviewers ask interviewees about a failure they learned from. When the interviewer does this, they are attempting to observe the emotions of the person they are interviewing as they recall the experience and draw the emotions of that experience out with it.

Help your teams recognize that it's okay to try things. It's okay to be wrong, and being wrong should not make them question their worth as employees or as people. Encourage them and help them continue to feel valuable and valued. By investing in your team in this way, you'll help them develop the ability to keep going in a state of Winner's Mentality, regardless of how their last sales opportunity went. You will see more lives changed and more sales as a result.

Intuition

The second characteristic, the empathetic skill of intuition, might be my favorite. The more intuitive we allow ourselves to be, the better we become at sales. This somewhat nebulous-sounding quality is actually a concrete skill that can be honed and measured as an improvement in closing ratio.

Being highly intuitive means being in tune with a deep sense of knowing—a gut feeling. We all have heaps of intuition—the question is, are we in tune with it? Some of the most powerful salespeople I know are very in tune with their intuition. It gives elite salespeople an edge that others struggle to identify, let alone hone and utilize.

To use intuition and improve in this ability, we have to choose to be in tune with all feelings. That's the funny thing about feelings—you can't pick and choose which ones you want to feel like some kind of buffet. It's all or nothing. Becoming adept at using intuition doesn't go well with being "tough," which some would consider a positive quality. However, tough and strong are not the same thing. The strongest people are both resilient and do not need to suppress emotions. They hold themselves responsible to interact well with their own feelings and the feelings of others. Their strength enables them to include feelings in the equation, which results in better choices. Simply being tough creates false simplicity and false freedom from the responsibilities that come with human emotions. Refusing to be in tune with something doesn't mean that it ceases to matter.

Consider this thought: The habit of suppressing emotions is produced by responding in fear. People suppress emotions because they fear vulnerability, judgment, losing control, or their darker feelings that might cause pain for others. It's normal to experience fear around those things, but there's a problem with that kind of normal. If I suppress feelings because I'm *feeling* afraid, that's still me being under the control of a feeling. Suppressing emotions out of fear is not the solution, and it ultimately only produces more intense pain because the suppressor of the feelings does not register the pain until it reaches critical levels.

Tenacity, too, is not the same as being tough. Tenacity is remaining adaptable while encountering challenges and moving forward anyway. Arrogant toughness is an exterior shell that feelings of inadequacy (and all your other feelings) hide behind. Let's be strong enough to notice our emotions, draw them out, express them in healthy ways, and help others do the same. I promise: you will see more lives changed and more sales made as a result of your team's heightened edge of intuition.

The strongest people treat their emotions like loyal servants. Strong people are in the driver's seat, with their goals set like a destination point on a GPS. Their emotions function like the lights and gauges on the dashboard. In this way, they're able to maintain awareness of things that otherwise might not be obvious. The gauges do not control our choices, they just inform our choices. That's how emotions work. Suppressing them is like ignoring the 'check engine' light because we don't like what it's saying.

There's nothing weak about emotional intelligence. Knowing which emotion you're feeling, where it comes from, what influences it, when to address it, how crucial it is and how it started are valuable things that elite salespeople pursue. In the process of acquiring this greater awareness, strengths like empathy, patience and gentleness are given space to develop. Sure, tuning awareness to recognize emotions means we'll be feeling more feelings, and that will be harder for some than others—but the harder it is, the more there is to gain.

Developing emotional intelligence will also give you the strength to set other people free. It doesn't just help the people who are around them; it also has a generational effect. It's just like a fitness lifestyle. In the pursuit of helping others become fit, we also become fit. In the pursuit of helping others find more emotional freedom, we will find more of it ourselves. The better we are at tuning into our own intuition, the more members we will have and the more lives we will change.

It's much easier to say, "I got _____ from my family members, it's just the way I was raised." It is much harder to say, "I grew up with someone who was angry. That motivated me to remove anger from my life forever." See, everyone and everything in our lives is either teaching us what to do, or what not to do. Ownership leaves no space for blaming our environment for what we do or don't have. It takes back our authority to influence that area. So, take ownership of your emotions, teach others to do the same, and change more lives as a result.

Here's a way to apply these thoughts on a very simple, practical level. I've taken on the helpful practice of pausing several times a day and asking myself, "How am I feeling?" Sometimes, the answer is just "hungry." Other times, it's frustration. Other times, it's tranquility. Tuning in to feelings means you'll notice all of them more. It might sound funny, but we might need to slow down to even realize that we're feeling feelings.

Why not test it out? First, recognize that you are and have been feeling one or several feelings for the past few hours. Second, give those feelings labels. Not "angry" or "happy" or "sad"—search until you find a precise term for one or more feelings that you're feeling. Then ask, "What kind of ___ is it?" Stop when you have a label with a description that is more detailed than is typical for you.

Finally, you're ready to learn more about that emotion. This is where exploration becomes useful. Use questions like:

- Where is this emotion coming from?
- What caused it?
- How long has it been around?
- Do I want more or less of this?
- What should I do in response to this?
- What should I do with it in the future?

This exercise will cause you to observe your emotions, rather than be controlled by them. Now, build that practice into your new habits. Make sure you believe that emotions are only an indicator that something needs to be attended to, and that they do not control you.

Dominion

Some will say with every strength comes a weakness. I would prefer to say that with every strength comes a responsibility. For instance, if a team member is highly intuitive and naturally a powerful listener, that strength comes with a responsibility: if they're not careful, they can become a doormat or even feel trapped on the roller coaster of other people's emotions.

However, attacking apparent "weaknesses" is not the way. Those "weaknesses" are just the fruit of failing to attend to the responsibilities associated with the strength. The responsibility held by the highly intuitive is to keep their own voice strong, to be sure of their own values, and remain confident in their own ability to impact their environment. Instead of attacking the weaknesses, build up areas of responsibility. The return for this effort is the ability for your salespeople to use their gifts in greater freedom by remaining healthy themselves.

The same concept of responsibility is true of dominant personality types. The potential weaknesses (self-centeredness, arrogance, or being seen as bossy and uncaring) are the fruit of failing to attend to the responsibilities associated with the strengths. The dominant person has the responsibility to think highly of others while also thinking highly of themselves. They have the strength to elevate those around them to their level and beyond, and they must choose to do so by recognizing that making others strong does not make them weak. The most powerful leaders do not collect subservient followers; they create more leaders and provide secure shoulders for their followers to stand on.

A healthy expression of dominion in the sales environment means that you have the ability to lead a prospect down a trail of discovery. Because of your confidence, care, and interest in helping others progress, you have the ability to ask questions that shed light on a current or future reality, even when it hurts. You help prospects have the gumption to look things in the eye that they wouldn't be able to without your support. You have authority in this area, but you do not carry the weight of the prospect's challenges.

Imagine you have an intuitive team member who's not developed in the area of owning their own authority. They spend some time with a prospect, asking questions, and discover that the prospect is forty-five pounds overweight, pre-diabetic, has high blood pressure and a low sex drive. Meanwhile, their husband is healthy, strong, and active. They maintain great rapport throughout the conversation with genuine care and concern. This team member, after pausing to absorb their reality, is feeling all the feels. Gently, they probe a bit further by quietly asking, "How long has it been since you felt great about your health in these areas?"

The prospect shares, "It's been a while. I guess I haven't felt great in some time. The last time would have been back in my mid-twenties."

Immediately, the heart of your team member goes out to this hurting person. Wanting to make it all better, the team member says, "That's okay, we're here for you and you're going to love it here! Don't feel bad about all that, because that is what brought you in. Everything is going to be better now! Our community is incredible and supportive, our classes are the best. We'll help you with nutrition too. It's only going to get easier and easier and easier! It's pretty tough to start, but I'll be here for you and make sure you achieve your goals."

Ultimately, the prospect never returns, and her life never changes, because the team member's empathy took over before the prospect made it across the finish line of internal change. Empathy and compassion alone are not enough to produce change in someone else's life. Gently invite your team to stop kissing butts and start changing lives. Help them let go of wanting to be seen as a nice person and set the standards higher. We aren't changing lives by temporarily soothing the self-inflicted wounds our prospects have caused themselves.

Financial commitment is the visible fruit of internal change. But in this first example, the motivator (the pain of remaining the same) was soothed in order to make the prospect feel better. That pulled the rug out from under all the motivation needed to overcome the pain of change. That temporary relief derailed this prospect's future success.

The team member's motivation for these soothing actions comes from a good place, but their actions are ultimately causing the prospect more long-term pain. Developing internal dominion to *use* our empathetic emotions instead of being *controlled* by them is what's needed here. With internal strength, a highly empathetic person does not slip into the role of a soother. Instead, they maintain the expert guide role in prospect conversations. With enough practice, your team will do that no matter how challenging it is. Here's the core of what caused everything to go wrong: emotions are powerful tools and wonderful servants, but they are all terrible masters.

Let's imagine that same situation again, but this time, your employee has developed the healthy characteristic of dominion. Now they are both empathetic *and* strong. No matter what any prospect shares, this team member maintains dominion over their own emotions. When that sneaky feeling pushes them to make it all better with soothing words, they know better. Instead of making someone feel better now, the team member makes the choice to press on. They also aren't attached to what the prospect thinks of them. They do what's best for the long-term health of the prospect, instead of what's best for their ego.

So, instead of soothing the prospect when she shares her woes, the team member asks questions like, "What would your husband say if you were to join a gym and start achieving the things you mentioned earlier?" or, "Earlier you said you haven't been very active since your mid-twenties. So how long have you been thinking about doing something about this?"

Instead of saying things that make the prospect feel like everything will be okay, the team member allows the tension between where the prospect is and where they'd like to be to remain. While the prospect feels the self-inflicted pain, the team member goes on to say, "Great, I can show you the membership options if you'd like. Which of these options do you think you might lean toward if you were to get started?"

This time, objections are less likely to arise, because instead of soothing her woes earlier, the salesperson allowed the tension to remain. They also asked good questions about how long the prospect had been thinking about taking action. They wanted to know what their husband would say before needing to address the objection. In this way, the most common objections were addressed before they surfaced. That way, they are less likely to get in the way of the sale—but if they do, your team will already be equipped.

However, let's say our prospect is a hard case and still presents the same objections because her habits are very ingrained. Her instincts are scrambling to find a way to maintain the safety of the old status quo. Instead of being a soother, the team member defaults into "guide" mode and gently isolates the objection. Then they remind the prospect of what they already said. "Didn't you say you have been thinking about changing for ten years, now? Is it really in your best interest to keep thinking about it, or would it be better for you to start feeling good about yourself?"

This time, there's a long pause. The prospect will break the silence after the last bits of their internal transition are complete. "You know what, let's do it!"

Healthy dominion means your team is strong enough to be the master of their own emotions. It means they press on, even if it produces short-term pain in exchange for potential long-term benefits. Notice you first must be able to master your own emotions before being able to help others overcome theirs.

This is a story for any of your team members who are hesitant to allow a prospect to feel the reality of their situation. Imagine if a surgeon was unwilling to exercise leadership in their area of expertise. There's a human in front of them under anesthesia who has a torn tendon that needs to be reattached. Everything is prepared but, just before surgery is to begin, the doc starts freaking out inside. His emotions run away with his mind. He says to the team of nurses, "I can't, I just can't cut this person open or encourage you to participate. I don't want to see any blood or cause them any more pain than they are already in."

That guy would lose his job. The surgeon wasn't being loving; they were acting out of a self-centered desire to be "nice." Instead of being the surgeon who's afraid of blood, let's exercise internal control. This will keep you out of the soothing mode and bring the strength that our prospects need. It is not our job to help someone feel good about their current situation if their current situation is not what they'd like it to be.

At the same time, we are not to push others around. The drive to do that is ultimately sourced in fear and weakness. Our role is to be strong enough to stop soothing the prospect's immediate emotional state and instead support their long-term health, without pushing. Bring the prospect to this mentality inwardly, and the external results will take care of themselves. Developing our own healthy, internal dominion as owners is what enables us to transfer this gift to our salespeople. Our salespeople then carry this gift forward into the lives of our future members.

The greatest of the Three Characteristics

Which of these traits matter most? Which is most important for sales? Some will say intuition, others will say dominion, but I will always say that *tenacity* is the most valuable and desirable quality. Edison said, "Many of life's failures are people who did not realize how close they were to success when they gave up." Tenacity is what keeps someone from giving up, even where dominion or intuition would fail.

Many highly intuitive people can be less likely to take dominant roles, out of fear. Enough pain can cause a highly intuitive person to pull back because they feel like they need to protect themselves.

Gym Membership Sales

Highly dominant personalities can be less likely to develop the more sensitive skills, also out of fear. Things like intuition are less likely to develop on their own. By seeking and accepting dominant roles, they are less likely to need to make progress by being sensitive to the wants and needs of others. A dominant person can also encounter intense enough pain to produce a massive shift out of dominion. Pain can cause a dominant person to react by lashing out or pulling back, potentially making them reclusive, among other things. By clamming up out of pain, over time, the interactive skills of intuition become forgotten.

Tenacity is inner resilience. It is what causes a person who encounters pain and fear to come back out of the shell and try again. Tenacity causes us to develop a balance of healthy dominion and intuition. Ultimately, intuition combined with dominion, laid on a foundation of tenacity, is what produces the most elite salespeople and life-changers.

Mastery of both intuition and dominion is arrived at by tenacity. Without tenacity, even the most intelligent and gifted will fail—but anyone can learn anything if they are tenacious enough.

Sealing the Deal on Your Success

"Rule with the heart of a servant. Serve with the heart of a king."
– Bill Johnson

This is only a book, so the rest will be up to you from here—but I can give you some coaching for the next leg of the journey. Nothing here will produce change in your life or the lives of those you serve without two things.

First, you must have a dedicated person running the business who's "all in." This means that the person at the helm is not running the business as a hobby or side gig. A hobbyist with excellent tools will lose to someone with mediocre tools who's all in. It doesn't matter how great the tools are if they aren't being used with the commitment of a professional.

Second, those who want results will need to take action. This book won't do anyone any good if they read this information and then do nothing about it. Absorb this information and do something with it. The thoughts and feelings we experience here are seedlings of new results that will fade fast without attentive cultivation, so make the choice now. Don't allow life to happen to you; instead, take ownership of your time and energy. You are not at the mercy of emotions or the demands of a busy schedule. You get to decide what you do with your life. It only takes one person who's willing to invest in creating more leaders in their business to start a generational ripple effect. You are the only one equipped for your role in this life. Go for it!

Final Thoughts

I have been unapologetically open with you about exactly what I think and believe to be right in this book. It's all based on what I use in the gym I own, what I've used in the gyms I've been part of that other people own and what I've personally consulted fitness franchisors and hundreds of gym and studio owners with. However, I'm not claiming to be 100 percent right about everything I've written here. This is just an acceptable representation of my best attempt so far. So, use my strategies and the thoughts we've shared here together as a catalyst to your own development. You don't have to start from scratch because you get to pick up the torch where others hand it off. The thing is, I'm not done running yet, so get everything you can from this book and the online resources and run *with* me.

There's one final pitfall to avoid for those of you who are taking action on what we've discussed here: Don't try to do everything. In order to realize the results you read this book in search of, you're going to need to take massive and imperfect action while moving methodically from one single priority at a time to the next. There's no such thing as "priorities" when we're talking about the development of a business, because if everything is important, nothing stands out. Discipline yourself to choose only one priority at a time. Keep the investment of your seconds, minutes, days, weeks, and months in alignment with long-term success markers. Each day, focus on the one main thing that will make the biggest difference in your business, and make time to reassess your investment of time and energy regularly.

Gym Membership Sales

Repeat this process until your business is built on reliable, simple systems that are easy to teach to others so that you don't have to do all of it for the rest of your life. In the fitness industry, that starts with being great at sales, retention and referrals—then you can successfully add great lead generation as fuel to the fire. In the beginning, you'll likely be the one doing those things, but as your business grows, your focus will shift from being great at sales, retention and referrals to being great at *teaching* those things. Once you're great at teaching the skills, your primary focus can move to intentionally cultivating the culture that produces sales and retention when you're not around. If you do something wrong in your business, don't let it be one of those things. With these foundational elements securely in place, you've got something worth building on and investing in.

By the way, do you remember the box trap I spent a lifetime on that summer when I turned eleven? Well, even though my dad didn't fix the trap for me that day like I had hoped, he gave me something much better than an easy fix. When he said to me, "Sometimes, the simplest solutions are the best," it set me on a journey to identify the most crucial elements of that little project and distill out the simplest possible solution. The results were a few new "pets" that summer. One of which bit my sister and several of which escaped in the house. I did end up having to get vaccinated for rabies eventually, and my mother had to outline a few new general "guidelines," but it all turned out pretty well for me that summer, and I saw the whole adventure as a great success.

In more recent years, I've re-learned that principle in some new ways and have observed that the best solutions to growing our gyms will not be found in elaborate schemes. Anyone can strap things onto things to create a complex house of cards... It takes a lot more tenacity and dedication to excellence to create the simplest possible solutions. Those are the solutions that are resilient enough to last a lifetime, and they are also the ones worth replicating.

I'd love to hear your thoughts on this book or what you got out of it. Also, if you want our help with having more leads, prospects, and members in your gym or studio with less effort from the most current resources available, let me know. Just send us a personal note telling us your thoughts on this book or what you'd like help with achieving to hello@membershipsalesbook.com. I will be happy to hear from you and the team and I would love to continue to support your success. Remember that you can access the online training and most current resources that go with this book here anytime: www. membershipsalesbook.com/resources

Finally, if developing as a person, growing your business and having more freedom is of interest to you, start finding ways of helping others have those things. This is the law of sowing and reaping. What we sow in the lives of others produces what we reap. It's the only reliable way to get more of anything, because we can't control what we get, but we can control what we give.

For some of you, the end of this book is only the beginning. I'm looking forward to hearing about your success!

I'll see you on the other side.

- Ryan

Made in the USA
Columbia, SC
24 February 2022

56789754R00090